Praise for *At An*

Do not begin to read *At Any Cost* as just another reading exercise. Mike and Hayley Jones understand well the cost of discipleship. They have encountered that cost, told in this incredible story of their adoption of eight siblings from Sierra Leone. Get ready for your life to be impacted by the radical message of the gospel. Get ready to laugh. Get ready to cry. And get ready to listen to the voice of God.

Thom S. Rainer, president and CEO of LifeWay,
and author of *I Am a Church Member*,
Autopsy of a Deceased Church, and *I Will*

As a coach you are always excited when one of "your guys" does something that makes you proud. This is especially the case with Mike Jones and his wife, Hayley. Their lives, love, commitment, and extraordinary faith come to life in *At Any Cost*. I encourage you to enjoy the blessing of reading it.

Phillip Fulmer, hall of fame coach and partner,
BPV Capital Management

One of the greatest things about God's calling on your life is knowing that He will always provide for whatever He's called you to. The Jones Dozen is a great example of God's calling and His provision.

Melinda Doolittle, artist and *American Idol* finalist

Mike and Hayley's story is an example of when God calls us to do something way beyond ourselves, He promises to equip us with everything we need to do it. While this story is about the Jones family and what God called them to do, it's one of those amazing stories that will speak to, inspire, and challenge all readers to listen to the Holy Spirit in a fresh new way.

Phil Joel, Christian musician and founder of deliberatePeople

Most of us will stand in awe as we are emotionally drawn through the picture frame on the front cover and into the lives of the Jones family. Sadly, many of us will miss it. The modern day miracle displayed in the lives of Mike and Hayley is not revealed in the incredible, extraordinary journey of adoption. No, their gift to each of us is discovered in their spiritual hearts that hear God speak; and their courageous hearts that step out in obedience.

Dewey Greene, author of *Painful Gifts* and
area chair at The C12 Group

God specializes in the impossible. That's what this book is all about. Mike and Hayley Jones relate their remarkable journey of three years to adopt eight children from Sierra Leone . . . but more than that it is a spiritual journey of their encounter with God along the way! This is a riveting story that has to be read.

Jimmy Draper, president emeritus, LifeWay,
and author of over 25 Christian books

"God moves in mysterious ways, His wonders to perform," an ancient poet wrote. Mike and Hayley Jones have lived this out as they prayed, waited, sacrificed, and trusted God to provide. *At Any Cost* will challenge your life to "wait on the Lord" and see the miracles He will provide.

Dr. Gerald L. Stow, ambassador,
Tennessee Baptist Children's Homes, Brentwood, Tennessee

It is so encouraging to hear God's people share their hearts with transparency and vulnerability. God has powerfully affected the hearts of Mike and Hayley through their call to adoption, and it has challenged us in all the right ways. *At Any Cost* is worth the read!

Ben and Julianna Zobrist, authors of *Double Play*

Buckle your seat belts! Get ready for an incredible journey of love and faith. If you follow the footprints of God, as Mike and Hayley Jones did, you will ride a roller coaster of emotion as you move from wondering *What in the world were they thinking?* to *Why not?*

Jim Henry, author, pastor emeritus,
First Baptist Church Orlando, Florida,
and former president of the Southern Baptist Convention

It has been a joy to witness the unfolding miraculous adventure of the Jones Dozen. *At Any Cost* is an inspiring story of faith, hope, love, and selfless dedication that is all too uncommon in our world today. Read this—better yet follow the Jones' example of loving the least, the last, and the lost of this world. It's a decision you'll never regret!

Steve Berger, author and senior pastor
of Grace Chapel in Leiper's Fork, TN

This isn't the story of soldiers and politicians. This is the story of a normal married couple with two normal children who had the courage to take God at His word. Because of their courage, the lives of eight orphans are forever changed. *At Any Cost* leaves us all haunted by the same question: What would be different if I found the courage to trust God?

Mike Glenn, author and senior pastor,
Brentwood Baptist Church

The Jones family has an incredible story of faith, perseverance, and family love. Their compelling, poignant, heart-warming story will resonate with anyone who has ever adopted—as well as those who are seeking to build a family that loves, prays, and sticks together through often funny, sometimes challenging circumstances. I highly recommend this book.

Wayne Hastings, author of *The Way Back from Loss*

In 2013, around Christmas time, I met Mike and Hayley Jones and their family. When I visited their home around this time, I was truly amazed by their story. Not only have they impacted people's lives by telling this story, but they have changed these children's lives forever. I admire and respect everything they have done—not only with these children's lives, but with staying strong in their faith and trusting in our Lord and Savior Jesus Christ.

Jalen Hurd, University of Tennessee running back

At *Any* Cost

At Any Cost

OVERCOMING EVERY OBSTACLE TO BRING OUR CHILDREN HOME

MIKE & HAYLEY JONES

WORTHY® PUBLISHING

Published by Worthy Books, an imprint of Worthy Publishing Group, a division of Worthy Media, Inc., 134 Franklin Road, Suite 200, Brentwood, Tennessee 37027.

WORTHY is a registered trademark of Worthy Media, Inc.

HELPING PEOPLE EXPERIENCE THE HEART OF GOD

eBook available wherever digital books are sold.

Library of Congress Cataloging-in-Publication Data

Jones, Mike (Michael W.)
At any cost : overcoming every obstacle to bring our children home / Mike Jones & Hayley Jones.
pages cm
Includes bibliographical references and index.
ISBN 978-1-61795-537-2 (paperback)
1. Jones, Mike (Michael W.) 2. Jones, Hayley. 3. Adoption--Religious aspects--Christianity. 4. Adoption--United States. 5. Intercountry adoption--Africa--Sierra Leone. 6. Adoptive parents--United States--Biography. 7. Christian biography--United States. I. Jones, Hayley. II. Title.
HV875.26.J66 2015
362.734092'39664073--dc23
2015010087

ISBN: 978-1-61795-537-2 (paperback)

Cover Design: Smartt Guys design
Cover Image: Adam Buzard

Printed in the United States of America
15 16 17 18 19 RRD 8 7 6 5 4 3 2 1

To our children, Michael, Samuel, Gabrielle, Levi, Malachi, Tyler, Judah, Isaiah, Zion, and Tucker. May our family's story bring glory to God.

And they overcame him by the blood of the Lamb,
and by the word of their testimony . . .

Revelation 12:11 KJV

Contents

Introduction

Everyone has a purpose. *Everyone* has a chance to fulfill it.

In 2013, our average American family of four grew to become the Jones Dozen by way of adopting eight siblings from a Sierra Leone orphanage. God took our new children's family tragedy and turned it into something beautiful. God, in His mercy and grace, led us to be a part of this miracle.

This book is not just our family's story, nor is it a how-to book on adoption. This is a book about redemption. It's also about listening to what God has called you to do and then being *all in* no matter how crazy or unrealistic it seems. It's about expecting God to work it out, keeping the faith, and knowing that when God says it's time, it *is* time, and no one can stop Him.

This book is not just our family's story, nor is it a how-to book on adoption. This is a book about redemption. It's also about listening to what God has called you to do.

When you listen and obey God's call, the journey will be hard, the valleys low, and the deserts almost unbearable. You may wander around the mountain for much longer than you expected. But even in the deepest, darkest places—when God is silent—He still *is*. There is a light somewhere ahead. So keep listening, keep believing, and He will come through in ways you could never imagine. You, too, will have a story to share.

No two stories are the same, just as no two people are the same. So don't compare our story with yours. Grab hold of your calling and run with it. Find peace where God puts you. Remember, God is writing your story, and He is limitless.

There will always be scoffers. Even gossipers. There will be those who whisper behind your back and those who may even yell in your face. But in the end there is only One to whom you must answer. Only One whose thoughts matter. He is God.

Writing is risky. God has done a great thing, but at times we wondered whether it was the best idea to write about it for the world. What if we're misunderstood? Once our story is in print, it's out there forever. This is true, but we have seen God move mountains, and "we cannot help speaking about what we have seen and heard" (Acts 4:20).

If this story gives just one person hope or changes one heart, it was worth the risk. Maybe that one person will be *you*. Our part is to tell the story; what you do with it is up to you.

—Mike and Hayley Jones

1

New Names

(Hayley)

I will praise you forever
for what you have done;
in your name I will hope,
for your name is good.
I will praise you in
the presence of your saints.

—

Psalm 52:9

Our day started early, as all days do in Sierra Leone. I woke at sunrise to the sounds of babies crying and children laughing and running up and down stairs to fetch water from the well. My guest apartment was in the middle of the orphan center, right in the heart of the action, surrounded by the great noise of one hundred kids. This place had become my second home as I spent weeks and even months at a time there over a heart-wrenching three years. But on that March morning in 2013, everything was new, and my joy was unspeakable. That day would bring a rebirth for eight children. Our children.

Later that afternoon the children and I said our goodbyes at The Raining Season orphan care center in Freetown. Then, we piled into taxis to leave the shelter they had lived in for the last three years. Five kids had been in the taxi with me, including our oldest, Melvin, who was fourteen, and Salieu, who bounced on my lap in the front seat.

That hot, ten-minute ride to the hotel was a weird, emotional time. As with many moments during the previous three years, I had felt like a spectator in my own life, as if

I were watching myself and all that was happening to me. While it was an exciting time for the kids, they had also just left their friends and everything they knew. We had ridden quietly, alone in our thoughts. Well, except for the little ones, who are never quiet. I was paying special attention to Melvin, calm in his seat, wondering what he was thinking. This child had seen into my soul the first time I met him.

As checked into the Family Kingdom hotel, I felt curious eyes on me, the white lady with eight African children. Speaking in Krio, the children excitedly talked about the slides they'd spied on the hotel's playground, the swimming pool, and the trampoline that was just like the one waiting for them at home. The hotel is a jewel in the middle of Freetown, the capital of one of the poorest nations on earth.

> For almost all of the three years we'd traveled, saved, cried, and waited to adopt these children, they continually asked us what their new names would be.

My eight children clambered past each other to get to the room first. Then we all paused at the door. The room was huge. It had four big beds, a couch with a coffee table, a desk, and a large bathroom. This hotel was the most amazing place they had ever seen. My heart smiled. I couldn't wait to show them more.

We were giddy as we plunked down our belongings. It was our final night in Sierra Leone. Mike and our boys, Tyler and Tucker, at home in Tennessee, were praying as they did every night that God would bring me home safely, this time with their brothers and sister.

My sweet daddy came in last, dripping sweat as he carried our suitcases and made sure no little ones had gotten lost along the way. He had flown in to meet me and help get his grandchildren home. I can't imagine what I would have done without him. The children ran around the room, jumping from bed to bed to feel the softness while others clicked and reclicked the TV buttons.

I wondered, *What should we do next? The playground? Dinner?*

No. First, they wanted their names.

For almost all of the three years we'd traveled, saved, cried, and waited to adopt these children, they continually asked us what their new names would be. None of us can remember exactly why they thought new names were a certainty that comes with adoption or when these conversations started, but now, after all we'd been through, new names made our new beginning even sweeter. The wait was over.

"Okay, Salieu, come on up," I said to the youngest. He popped up off the couch and stood next to me while seven other pairs of eyes expectantly waited and watched. This was finally happening. This moment couldn't have been any more perfect, any more special. And, it couldn't have meant any more to me.

"We're all adopted children of God. God adopted us all," I told them as they sat around the couch. "We all get a new beginning. We get a fresh start. We never forget our past. We always cherish it, and we always remember the good memories because they are forever part of us and what made us who we are," I said. "But there's a time when we can start something new and move on from things that were bad or from things you don't like. You can become a new person; you can be who you want to be. So it's a new start for everybody."

I slowly looked into the face of each precious child around me. This moment was one of those little things along the way that felt right. I could sense God smiling down. "One of the great things about it taking so long to get you guys home is that we got to pray and choose names that really fit your personalities. We chose all biblical names because we know you're God's children, and the only reason we have you is because of Him.

"Your first name is Zion," I said as I looked into four-year-old black eyes that had already seen so much. "The Bible says Jesus will return for His people in the end on Mount Zion," I read from the papers I'd prepared for each child with their photos and the meaning of his or her name.

"You are the youngest, the end of our Great Eight. You are strong and beautiful. For these reasons, we chose this name for you."

All eight children yelled and clapped and jumped up and down for Zion's new name.

My daddy sat off to the side trying not to cry. He teared up, pulled out his handkerchief, and pushed up his glasses. Most of the children's middle names are family names, with several of them from my dad's side. He was very proud, and it was sweet watching him. Ask Daddy about that moment now and he still chokes up. "They're just special kids," he says.

Zion's middle name is Davidson, the surname of his great-grandparents.

"Your middle names are family names because now you have an even bigger family and even more people who love you. I wanted to make sure you always feel and know you're part of this one big family."

Over those years of waiting, whenever the children asked Mike and me about their names, we'd say we didn't know yet and were praying about it. And then we'd change the subject. Because it wasn't time. But two weeks earlier, right before I left to come to Sierra Leone to hopefully bring our children home, Mike and I finally decided on their new names.

For years God had been weaving this tapestry, redeeming

all of our lives. Redeeming heartache. He had watched over these children; He had guarded and protected them. The fact that they are alive and well was a miracle from Him. We knew these children belonged to Him, and we wanted their names to reflect that.

I called up Alusine. At six, he was a ball of energy. "Your first name is Isaiah, which means 'the Lord helps me.' The Lord has helped you and watched over you and us." His middle name is William, the name of his grandfather and two great grandfathers.

Next was Victor, our seven-year-old. "Your name is Judah. We praise the Lord for you. Your strength is one of the reasons we gave you this name." Currell, his middle name, was his great-grandfather's name.

They yelled, jumped up and down, and clapped. Every time. I probably could have said any name and they would have screamed. Their reactions were priceless.

As I looked around the room at all their sweet faces, I saw the backpacks I had given them strewn about. I still smile when I think about how many times at home I'd packed and unpacked each backpack with a toothbrush, toothpaste, pajamas, underwear, socks, and an outfit to wear home to America. When we were leaving the center, I told them to pack anything they wanted to bring home. But, there wasn't anything. They had some clothes, some of which we'd sent earlier, and a few African clothes I'd had made by a vendor at the Freetown market. They had tried for a while to keep a few sentimental possessions, but most things there tend to get lost or taken. It was sad, especially for the older ones. They had nothing to show from the first dozen or so years of their lives. All they had was in those backpacks.

"Mohammed," I called to our next child. I looked him in the eyes and told him, "Your name is Malachi. It means 'messenger of God.'" At eight, he could quote more scripture than anyone we knew. He would ride around the orphan center on a bike reciting Bible verses. I said, "You are a messenger of God!" His middle name is Drake, my maiden name. My father's last name. And, out came Daddy's handkerchief again as he pushed up his glasses.

I didn't cry. I was so excited, and I wanted to soak in the moment, catch every detail as I watched their faces. I didn't want my emotions to get in the way. Was our struggle actually over? Was this real? Were our three years of heartache to bring our Great Eight home finally at an end?

"Peter." My nine-year-old. "Your name is Levi. It means 'pledged' or 'joined.' You are now joined to our family." He's our artist, and they say people with this name tend to be creative. We kept Peter as his middle name. The rock. Jesus named His apostle Peter the rock of the church.

Kadiatu, our princess and our only girl, was eleven. "Your name is Gabrielle. Woman of God." Her faith and prayers during those years showed she is a true woman of

God. Grace is her middle name, which is the name of her great- grandmother. Oh, His amazing grace and favor.

Yusufu was thirteen. "Your name is Samuel, which means 'God heard.'" How much we had prayed for him and God had answered. We chose his middle name, Titus, which means "pleasing," because of his gentle, loving spirit.

In the days to come, if I got mixed up and used their birth names, which I'd been calling them for three years, I was quickly corrected, believe me.

And, finally, our oldest, Melvin. "Your name is Michael, the angel warrior, the leader." He loved that. He really claimed that name. At fourteen, he was a natural leader and had led his brothers and sister for years (and now leads all nine of them). As our oldest, he also shares the name of his father. His middle name is Thomas, after great-uncles on both sides of our family.

Oh, they loved their new names and never once said they wished for something else. They studied their own papers, which I later collected for safekeeping. In the days to come, if I got mixed up and used their birth names, which I'd been calling them for three years, I was quickly corrected, believe me.

After a chicken dinner at a restaurant next door, the kids

couldn't get enough of the soccer game on TV. They were fascinated and took hundreds of pictures of the TV with my phone. They had their first hot showers. My dad stood in the bathroom with groups of them, instructing how to wash faces first, then body parts. With his clothes soaked, he laughed out loud as he opened the bathroom door and I watched steam roll out along with my wet kids.

We fit two or three to a bed, and I felt the cool breeze from the only air conditioner I had felt in the last two weeks. Still, the familiar smell of heat and humidity pressed through the hotel window, and my emotions were so strong that I worried they may be heard. Surely the other hotel guests could hear my heartbeat through the walls.

This is it, I said to myself as I checked the time on my phone. I looked over the passports again . . . still eight, just as there had been five minutes earlier. I recounted the giant, sealed, white envelopes given to me by the U.S. Embassy. Waves of peace, complete and utter perfection, rushed over me. Only God had gotten us here. No one could ever imagine what He had done for me this final week and what He had shown me. When He says the time has come, then the time has come. There is nothing anyone can do to stop it. God had proven that to me.

Mixed with the gratitude came a darkness and a fear that I still cannot adequately put into words. Thoughts raced through my mind: *What if we get stopped at the airport?*

What if the government chases me down, changes its mind about our adoption, and won't let us go? What if my children are not allowed to come home? Again, I checked the time, counted the passports, and flipped through the envelopes.

I studied the children lying in the beds and pleaded silently to them. Here we all are. Together. We are going home. No more sad good-byes. No more leaving my children in an orphanage in a third-world country. No more "let's keep praying" for God to move the mountains. He has done it. Now is the time to rejoice, to praise Him. Children, remember this. Think of it often. Breathe in this moment and taste it. Never stop thanking Him for this. No matter what the future holds and what happens in your lives, this is a moment when God gave you victory. Hold on to it.

2

The Journey Began Years Ago

(Hayley)

I will not leave you as orphans;

I will come to you.

—

John 14:18

As a girl, I dreamed of being a missionary in Africa. If I saw something on TV about Africa, it mesmerized me. Maybe it was the adventure and the challenge that called to me from my comfortable home in Franklin, Tennessee. I don't know where this deep love for Africa originated. I just know I feel it. Even before I ever set foot on that big continent, I felt a longing deep down in my soul for it. When I first landed in Sierra Leone, that longing became a peace. I can't put this peace into words, but I feel it every time I am there.

When I visited Sierra Leone, time was passed meeting the needs of others. Days consisted of surrendering to God and allowing Him to use me to help. It can be overwhelming, all the need; that's why you really have to listen to God and let Him guide you. I could go crazy and broke trying to figure out what to do and meet every need, so I quickly learned that needs will always be plenty, and I certainly cannot meet them all. But I must do my part. That's all I have to do . . . my part. My prayer when I'm there is simply, "Use me, God." I learned that when I feel like I am being poured out is also when I feel the most complete. Surrendering and letting go made me feel so strong and so humble. When I was emptied of myself, there was plenty of room for Jesus to fill me up.

When I was little, Mom says I was very sensitive, stopping her to pray if we heard an ambulance siren. So early on God had fertile ground in me to plant the seed to love Africa and, over the years, to water it. My older sister felt the call too. She and her husband and five children lived in South Africa for over four years as missionaries. Our middle-class upbringing was wonderful, yet typical, and my parents still marvel at what God has done in their girls' lives.

God also worked on Mike. From a young age, Mike had always thought he'd adopt a boy from Africa. He doesn't recall ever telling his parents or brother; it was a sense of something he would do later in life to fulfill a purpose. God was preparing him for adoption when he barely understood the concept of adoption and he didn't know anyone who had been adopted. Even so, he was very confident he would adopt a little boy from Africa. Funny how God knows exactly how to prepare us, one idea at a time. (Seven boys and a girl! Well, that He would reveal later.)

God sparked these little fires in us that we stoked as we dated and shared our dreams. Years later, after our first child, Tyler, was born, Mike and I restarted the adoption conversation, wondering what it might look like for our family. We considered adopting from Ethiopia and even got the paperwork for it. But, the papers sat because we didn't feel peaceful about it. Five years later, when our second son, Tucker, was a year old, we got serious and looked into different adoption agencies. At that time we considered South Africa because our church had a ministry there. But once again, nothing felt right.

People still ask me, "Why not adopt here in the United States?" Well, that wasn't our call. One kind of adoption is not more right than another kind. It's like asking someone, "Why aren't you a doctor? Don't you know there are so many sick people in the world?" Mike says that God calls us to certain places. For us, that place was Sierra Leone, a place that will always hold a part of my heart. And we knew that God was calling us to adopt.

Satan literally fights like hell to keep orphans suppressed, making them feel unwanted and unneeded at all times. He desires nothing more than to keep the orphan from feeling loved. Christ intends for a child to be loved by a father and mother and be raised in the likeness of Christ and be taught His ways. Mike and I know we're all God's adopted children. Psalm 68:4–6 says it all.

> Sing to God, sing praise to his name,
> extol him who rides on the clouds—
> his name is the Lord—

and rejoice before him.
A father to the fatherless, a defender of widows,
is God in his holy dwelling.
God sets the lonely in families.

God is always busy in the details of our lives, orchestrating the meetings, the intersections that could open doors now or down the road. Early in my teaching career, I had a sweet child in my kindergarten class who had been adopted from Sierra Leone. A casual conversation with her mom, Erica Stone, at a parent-teacher conference would stay tucked in my heart until it was God's time to act on it. She told me to call her when I was ready and said she'd love to share their family's story. Now was the time. I told Mike I knew I had to talk to Erica. I'd saved her phone number for about seven years, but her number had changed. I had an idea of where they lived, but no address. For two or three weeks, she stayed on my mind.

God is always busy in the details of our lives, orchestrating the meetings, the intersections that could open doors now or down the road.

One day a free community newspaper we randomly received a few times a year landed in our driveway. There she was. The paper had a story about Erica's family, their adoption, and an orphans' shelter they had recently opened in Sierra Leone. And there was her phone number. That was the sign I needed. I stood in the driveway and did a little squeal. I called Mike immediately and said, "You're not gonna believe this!" The time had come, and this was what we had to pursue.

Excitement and nerves bubbled up as I called Erica that day. Unbelievably, she remembered our brief conversation about adoption years earlier. Within a week, she was sitting at my kitchen table telling me about her three-year ordeal to adopt her sweet girl. After adopting, she and her husband felt God's push to do more in Sierra Leone. A few months before our meeting, they had opened The Raining Season in Freetown to care for orphaned children physically and spiritually and to give them an education. The center had been set up to keep families together amid bleak poverty but had become an orphanage.

In the mid-1990s, UNICEF and other international organizations redefined an orphan as a child who has lost one or both parents. A third-world child does not have to lose both parents to be considered an orphan, as would be the case with our children. The change in terminology came as AIDS claimed millions of parents and left kids destitute in the care of only one parent or grandparent. Today, an estimated twelve thousand children are Ebola orphans, having lost one or two parents or a primary caregiver to the horrendous virus (unicef.org). When we hear a statistic like that, we know to assume it's underestimated because many deaths, especially in villages, are regularly not recorded.

Sierra Leone, a West African coastal country with six million people, is just a little smaller than South Carolina. It's an incredibly hard place for a child, and nearly a fifth of children don't make it to age five. Literacy is low, and left-overs from decades of unrest and civil war in the 1990s hurt the economy. Poverty is rampant. In fall 2014, the country had the highest number of Ebola cases, eclipsing other West African countries.

This was the country that would capture our hearts.

As Erica left my house that spring day in 2010, God gave me clarity and purpose. This was the organization. There was no doubt. Mike and I both knew it. We don't sit on decisions for long, whether it's about big things like getting married or little things like buying a lawnmower. "Let's jump in with both feet and get this thing done," Mike said. Our prayers felt clear, unburdened, and excited. "God, this is it. Show us what's next." We were clueless about the time it would take to realize these dreams and prayers. We just assumed that if God opened the door, we'd run in.

We loved what The Raining Season was fighting to do there. But we knew, too, that we had to seek God's face about this. Our plans were to adopt a child. But was that God's plan? Mike and I spent the next week or two praying over our decision, and we shared our hopes with Tyler, then four, who joined in our prayers after baby Tucker was in bed. "Should we be sponsors for children at the center? Should we plan on mission trips? Is it adoption, Lord, like we think it is?"

I talked to Tyler about adoption one night while putting him to bed. Every night we would read Bible stories. After reading to him, I scratched his back and we talked about how God calls everyone to help the widow and the orphan. I read him James 1:27: "Religion that God our Father accepts as pure and faultless is this: to look after orphans and widows in their distress and to keep oneself from being polluted by the world." I told him it was time Mommy and Daddy did something about that. I asked him to pray with us that God would show us exactly how He wanted us to help. That night and every night that week Tyler prayed for God to tell us how to help the widow and the orphan. To show us what to do. God answered with a quiet reassurance and peace. Adoption was our call.

3

Wrestling with God

(Mike)

Yet the LORD longs to be gracious to you;
he rises to show you compassion.
For the LORD is a God of justice.
Blessed are all who wait for him!

—

Isaiah 30:18

I'd love to say that I've always listened to God's voice and obeyed. Truth is, God met me where I was several years ago and worked on me anyway. I have been in church since the cradle and got saved when I was nine. Often people who come to faith like that become numb to His voice. We always attended church—every Sunday, every Wednesday night—but for a time I forgot how to listen and how to really seek God. I just assumed He was always there. But I've always loved Him. Even when I was doing my own thing, a deep reverence stayed buried in my heart.

The Holy Spirit wasn't something we talked much about growing up in Nashville in our Baptist church. After I was saved, I always thought that little voice or feeling was an odd case of women's intuition; at least that's what I called it. But that little voice *is* the Holy Spirit. We're born alive, but not alive with God. When I got saved, I was born again with the Holy Spirit, who brought me back to life in God. Accepting Jesus Christ as Lord and Savior meant I have a relationship with Him. So when I pray, I can have a conversation with my heavenly Father. It's not about saying grand, elaborate, wordy prayers, but small, simple prayers. It's a talk with Dad.

When I was eighteen and nineteen, living a few hours away from home at college, I let loose and spread my wings. At the University of Tennessee, I was a walk-on wide receiver for the 1996 and 1997 seasons when Peyton Manning was quarterback. I was blessed to play on the team that won an SEC Championship with dozens of guys who went on to have careers in the NFL. Beyond the field, I fell to the bottom. I'd fight anyone who looked at me the wrong way, and I partied late into the night most days of the week. That new sense of freedom, having no curfew as I had had at home, and my lack of maturity made for disaster. There was always something to do, and I was game to do it. I chose not to hang out with Christian football players, and there were a bunch. Instead, I chose the party crowd. It was definitely my prodigal son experience. God had given me an opportunity, but when the road split I ran down the wrong path.

I left UT in January 1998. Shin splints turned into stress fractures that needed about six months to heal. That's the reason I could tell people about why I was leaving. But I also knew I wouldn't play football beyond college, and most importantly I knew I wasn't living my life with Christ. The real reason I left was my sin. In those wild times, I had cheated on my long-time girlfriend back home, and the Holy Spirit convicted me to tell her. Her hurt devastated me even more.

I had caused hurt and pain for my own selfish gain. That realization of my selfish sin caused me to grow up. That hurt should never and will never again happen to the one I love.

Sin has consequences. Leaving school meant I was also no longer part of the team that would go on to win a second SEC championship and a national championship during the 1998 season. Instead, I returned to my heavenly Father. I became intentional about dating, and God would bless me with meeting Hayley a short time later. After I came home, I focused strictly on academics and finished my degree at Middle Tennessee State University. I also began seeking the Holy Spirit's guidance.

As a kid, I had always felt that someday I would adopt a boy from Africa. God had pressed that on my heart. Of course, I had no idea what that would look like or how it would happen. It was just a deep-down feeling. After our early marriage struggles (more about that later), Hayley and I drew close to God. He reassured us and made us stronger as a couple. Within a few years, I became a deacon at church. We eventually went to another church where Hayley joined the choir, which she

> I was blessed to play on the team that won an SEC Championship with dozens of guys who went on to have careers in the NFL. Beyond the field, I fell to the bottom.

loved. We enjoyed our activities, our lives, and our kids, but we quietly yearned for more. We weren't complaining or becoming dissatisfied with life, but something was missing.

In 2010, we decided that we would adopt from Sierra Leone and that hole started to fill. But we both felt like God was telling us to do more and to think bigger. More. We would do more. I was out of my comfort zone and drawing closer to God again, seeking His face about what to do. What was *more*? In those few weeks after our resolve to adopt was clear, we let Erica know we were thinking about adopting more than one child. She had mentioned a brother and sister, and another sibling group of four that included a set of twins. We set up another meeting with Erica and vaguely had the larger group in mind. We met on a Friday for a long lunch to talk about the adoption process and how it would work. She showed us sibling groups of two and three who were living at The Raining Season and said, "Well, that's about it." And then I pointed to a tablet she'd set to the side. "What are these names over here?"

"Well, we have a group of six and a group of eight," she said.

BAM! It was like I got hit in the head with a hammer. "A group of eight." I physically felt a sharp, painful blow. *That's it. The Eight*. It all happened so fast, it was as if it were happening to someone else. But, no, it was me. This was real. And I knew that breathtaking, painfully clear thought could only come from God. I don't remember anything that was said for the rest of our meeting. I didn't let on to either Hayley or Erica what had just happened. My mind raced as we got up to leave.

As I drove Hayley back home, my wheels turned faster than those on our car. I said, "Don't bother Erica now, but she never showed us that group of four. Let's wait till Monday and ask her about them." I was already trying to bargain and trade with God. Before that moment, when we knew God was telling us to do *more*, I'd thought adopting four children would be impossible. That sounded like too many. So, I never asked Erica about the four because I knew I couldn't take care of four more kids. But after God showed me eight children in that blinding moment, I was already trying to backpedal into four. Four sounded good now. *That could be the "more." Right, God?*

I mentioned them again to Hayley that Sunday night. "Don't forget to ask her about those four." She did, and we got some information. But I knew that wasn't what we were supposed to do. I kept quiet about the eight; I couldn't say a word to Hayley yet. God had to confirm that direction to me some other way. I needed Him to give me a sign.

I could barely sleep for the next week or two. I was irritable and would bicker about nonsense if Hayley tried to ask me what was wrong, and then I'd blame my mood on work. I felt sick when I tried to eat. I went to work and kept up appearances, but just couldn't do anything except roll it over in my mind. *There's no way in the world*, I'd think. *Who would do that? I can't do that, God. Four has got to be it. I'll do the four. I can't afford eight. How are we supposed to manage logistically?* None of it made sense.

I'd had life planned out. I look back now and laugh at how much I thought I had figured everything out until all this happened. Hayley and I would sit down and make our budget work for what we set out to do. I had begun working at Milcrofton, a water utility district here in Middle Tennessee, and I'd think, *When I became general manager, we'll be able to go on trips when we want and buy what we need. Maybe we'll eventually have a lake house or something.* I'd always wanted a Hummer, like an H1, an old army-type diesel Hummer. My mind now went in so many directions. With four more children, I knew my plan wasn't going to happen. But maybe some version of it could still happen. *It would be a whole lot easier with four than it would be with eight, right? I mean, who in their right mind . . . ? Eight? No!*

Hayley, meanwhile, was pumped after our meeting with Erica and loved learning about children at The Raining Season center. One day she was sitting at the kitchen table with her laptop, looking at children's photos and thinking about which ones might join our family. She thought about what it would be like to be their mother. Then a sick feeling settled into the pit of her stomach. She thought, *Who do I think I am to "pick" a child? What gives me the right to say I want that child? No way. I can't do this.* She closed the laptop with sweet faces of children on the screen and said out loud, very matter-of-factly, "God, if You want me to adopt a child, You will have to show me which one. I will not choose." She immediately felt relief. God had this.

She said nothing to me about this at the time, but she was right. God had it all right. For about two weeks, I struggled like I've never struggled in my life. I tried to force myself to appear as though everything was okay, but I was torn up inside. I constantly thought about the eight when I was in the truck going to a job site or while praying in the morning or at night. If I had a moment when I wasn't completely engulfed in something I was doing or working on, I was thinking about the eight. I knew nothing about that list of kids. Were they boys? Girls? Special needs? There was no rest. I begged God to speak. *Tell me more! I'm not just going to do this based on some feeling of getting hit in the head*, I'd pray. *If You really want this, You're going to have to tell me more!*

My fidgeting and short temper were driving Hayley nuts, but she pretty much left me alone, figuring I'd talk when I was ready to talk. One Sunday I went to church hoping to get filled up and find some peace. We sat in a pew in the center aisle, halfway up. A safe spot where we could see well but blend into the crowd. We sang the songs, gave our offering, and tried to listen to the pastor. But I was wriggling like a worm on a hook. I put my arm around Hayley for a minute, but I couldn't stay still and I almost jumped to shift in my seat. Hayley shot me a look and silently mouthed, "What is wrong with you?" No peace. No word from God. I actually got up and left the service before the pastor delivered the sermon. I walked up and down the halls of the church and tried to not look like a crazy person, but I was eaten up!

After Tyler and Tucker were in bed that night, Hayley went to take a shower. I couldn't take this struggle any longer. Sitting on the bed, I started praying, and then I decided to kneel down and get serious about it. Somehow I wound up turned against the wall, my face on the floor. I can't relive this moment now without choking up. "God!" I cried out loud. "This is too serious. You've got to tell me something. I know what You want me to do, but I just can't do it. I can't provide for them. You have to show me. Tell me something! I can't keep on like this. I'm miserable, I'm consumed, I'm choked, I can't do it!"

> "God, I can't do this," I cried. "There's no way I can feed that many." I heard God so very clearly: I can feed twice as many. *This is what you must do.*

I was facedown on the floor, praying, but I was going somewhere else. Into His presence. It was dark all around me, but He was illuminated. All I could see were His feet and His legs from the knees down. I was like a kid trying to grab at the feet of his daddy. He had come down to me. This wasn't heaven. He came to me! God had compassion for me and was going to set me straight. I remember trying to wrap myself around Him and grab hold as if I could hold Him and plead to Him, change His mind, not surrender to His will.

"God, I can't do this," I cried. "There's no way I can feed that many. Let me do the four. I can take care of the four, but I can't do the eight."

I heard God so very clearly: *I can feed twice as many. This is what you must do.*

And that was it. I was back there on my bedroom floor. Peace. Quiet. I knew right then that those eight children were mine. I never questioned it again.

Hayley finished her shower, and I sat on the bed, waiting. "I've got to talk to you." I had been so miserable because I thought I had to do it all, to provide for my family. But God clearly told me He was going to take care of us. Not four more children, but twice as many. He would take care of the eight. He would take care of all twelve of us. This wasn't about Mike Jones but about God Almighty!

Talking and crying, I told Hayley how God had spoken to me at the meeting with Erica two weeks earlier. I told her I knew right then that those eight children were ours, but

I couldn't live with it and tried to deny it. I told her how I'd been trying to barter and dicker with God to find some other way. I told her about how I had begged Him to tell me something specific if He wanted me to go out on faith like this, because I didn't have faith like that! I was not a pastor; I was not some well-studied, on-fire follower of Christ leading souls to the kingdom. I was a nobody!

"We're supposed to adopt that group of eight," I choked out.

Hayley had been waiting for an answer from God, so her response to me wasn't the flipped-out one you'd expect. She just asked, "So how did you get to this?"

"I was on my knees, trying to hold on to God, Hayley," I tried to explain. "And He plainly told me He would take care of us. I've got a complete peace about it. And this is what we've got to do." I no longer thought the idea was crazy, doubted it, or questioned how. It was just what must be done. Those were our kids.

Hayley smiled. "I've been waiting for you to tell me." And she told me about closing her laptop, unable to choose a child, telling God to show her. Hayley will say that I've never cried in my life until these children entered our lives. She knew something had happened to me. This broken, emotional man just wasn't me. God broke me. Completely. He changed my heart and my spirit. Hayley says God knew He had to get to me first. If she'd come to me crying about adopting eight kids, I probably would have rolled my eyes and said, "Hayley, seriously?"

She knew only God could have changed this man and broken his heart for what breaks His. "Then that's what we have to do," she said. "This is it." No more panic. A complete answer from God. It was obvious. And from that point on, we never looked back. We would cling to this moment in the dark days ahead, remembering how God was so clear and peace was so abundant.

4

Going Separate Ways

(Mike)

Now to him who is able
to do immeasurably more than
all we ask or imagine,
according to his power
that is at work within us.

—

Ephesians 3:20

Some twelve years before that life-changing moment before God, when Hayley was a senior in high school, I met her at church. I knew her older sister, Courtney, from UT, because she was dating my friend Joey. Hayley was so young that I didn't really think about dating her. Besides, I was busy with college classes at MTSU and working on our family farm. But her mom took me aside one day after church. "I just want to let you know that Hayley likes horses too," she said. "If you ever want to ask her to ride, that would be okay." She was pretty much telling me to ask her daughter out. As we were leaving church, I told my brother, "Well, that was kind of weird."

But I did ask if she wanted to come riding, and Hayley, who wasn't thinking much about me either, said, "Oh, yeah, I like horses." She came over to my parents' farm, and we rode and talked. It was fun, and an easy friendship started, but I was still thinking she was too young to date. I was a sophomore in college, and after my experiences at UT, I'd put up an emotional wall. But I asked her to my parents' house again, and I cooked fish for dinner and then we drove around the farm. After that second time together, I saw the maturity in her and my wall started crumbling. She was fun, vibrant, and beautiful. She had skipped her junior year of high school and was on her way to graduating early, so she didn't fit in with high school girls at church and met with the college group instead.

There was something special about her. It wasn't a giddy, fluttery love that developed between us but just a knowing. Within a few months, I knew she was the one. We started dating in late fall, and she was a little surprised when I gave her a Christmas gift: a CD and some earrings from one of my parents' trips to Santa Fe, New Mexico. My mom gave her a devotional book, *Experiencing God*, which she read and really took to heart.

I had lived through my wild stage of life (Hayley laughs when she thinks of that, saying she would not have been interested in me back then), but after we had been dating about five or six months, I asked her parents if I could marry her. I proposed where we started—on a horse ride. We stopped at the top of a hill between two trees, and I got down on one knee and pulled the ring out of my Wrangler jeans' pocket. She was totally shocked, but she said yes.

That was April of her senior year. We married just four months later in August before she started college, and I continued my junior year. It wasn't a huge wedding, but as Hayley says, "It was perfect." She's not a big to-do person and says now we should have just eloped and saved the money. We honeymooned at a condo in Florida that my parents owned at the time.

I turned twenty-one during our honeymoon. Hayley was still seventeen and needed to get permission from her parents to marry. If you asked us now if someone that age should get married, we would say no. But, well, we did.

My parents and hers knew it was important that we both finish college. Commuting to different colleges, I was working to finish my degree in agriculture business and also would get a minor in business administration. Hayley started working on her elementary education degree and worked at a home goods store. We lived in a nine-hundred-square-foot loft above a four-car garage on my parents' farm. I worked for my dad at the farm raising cattle, earning eighteen thousand dollars a year, which paid for our tuitions, fuel, horse expenses, and little else. Do we buy milk or orange juice this week? Not both. If we buy cereal, then we have to buy milk. But if we get Pop Tarts, we can get orange juice instead.

Once the newness of marriage wore off, it drove Hayley crazy that our apartment really wasn't a home. We had a mini fridge, a microwave, and a sink, but no stove, so she couldn't cook. She wanted to be able to relax at home, but our place felt so temporary, not homey at all. Most nights we had dinner with my parents. Within about a year, we were able to move to another house on the farm, which was much better.

We stayed busy and really didn't see each other much. That's when the problems started. The stress from long days, school, work, and living week to week on nothing ended with us bickering about stupid things. Little things. And our biggest problem: God was an afterthought.

My temper flared often over little things. I was harsh. I'd complain in front of people about something Hayley did or didn't do. I was sarcastic and said mean things I never should have said. I definitely wasn't building her up. It's absolutely no excuse, but I didn't know any better. For me, I didn't think much about snapping like that. But for Hayley, it was belittling. She felt smaller and smaller, like she could not do anything right. She lost her confidence. She was so young and would say now that she just didn't know who she was. It was a bad time. During the short time we dated, she'd never seen me angry. Now, that was all she saw.

Adding to the stress was a new business project for our farm that my dad and I were creating following my college graduation, something built around my passion: showing and training horses. But to make that work financially, we decided to board horses too. That wasn't part of my dream, but I felt pressure to make that business work. Life became constant work, stress, and bickering. All the little things snowballed into big things, and Hayley and I couldn't talk without fighting. About our lack of money, about dinner, about who knows what. Hayley might say something, then I'd yell, and then instead of arguing with me, she would just shut down. That made me feel ignored, so I got more upset. Hayley, true to form, didn't say half of what was really on her mind. She climbed into her turtle shell.

> The stress from long days, school, work, and living week to week on nothing ended with us bickering about stupid things. Little things. And our biggest problem: God was an afterthought.

We hid our troubles. Or, at least we thought we did. We didn't talk to my parents or hers about the struggles we were having. They could see glimpses but really didn't know the depth of it. We went to a huge church where it was easy to go to the service and leave. We got our little taste of God for the week and had no connections there at all except for family. I eventually started snapping at Hayley in front of her sister, Courtney, and her husband, Joey, who had married a few months after we did. I even snapped at her in front of her parents. Hayley tried to laugh it off in front of them to cover it up, but they saw. I just didn't care. I was miserable. She was miserable.

Our upbringings were different in how we dealt with

conflict. Hayley wouldn't argue back with me; she'd give in or shut down. I didn't want her to give in. I worked stuff out with yelling. But that wasn't her way. When we were dating and still had that young love glow, it was blissful. We never even had a disagreement; everything was perfect. We couldn't imagine these rough roads, and we weren't prepared to handle them.

I thought, *So, this is it? This is life? There has got to be more*. After about three years of marriage, I told Hayley, "We should just get a divorce." I printed legal forms I'd found online and showed her. We went to the pastor, somehow expecting him to bless our divorce. It was crazy. He didn't, of course. We didn't seek his advice either. I don't know if I would have listened anyway. I told Hayley I didn't want her anymore and that she had to leave. I was cold and hateful. At twenty, still in college, Hayley put her foot down. "No. I'm not leaving," she'd said. "Where am I supposed to go?" She moved out of our bedroom and slept upstairs. We barely spoke, brushing by each other in the kitchen to get food.

I worked a lot, and with Hayley in college or working, we could avoid each other. After about four months of that miserable existence, Hayley had had enough. Once her parents moved into their new house, Hayley had her solution. She took the dog and left. It was officially over. No more trying to hide it. I told my parents we were separated. They were devastated and urged me to fight for the marriage. I didn't know it then, but they stayed up all night praying for us.

Hayley's parents knew she had been sleeping upstairs, so they weren't completely surprised when she showed up at their door. She stayed in her parents' front bedroom and kept on going to school. She told her parents just enough, but she didn't really confide in them, much to their dismay. To her, there was nothing to talk about. It was over. Her parents' house was a safe place to land, but it wasn't peaceful. She felt lost. All of her friends were getting engaged or off having fun at college. Hayley has never been one to hang out at clubs, so she met a few friends for dinner on occasion, but mostly she stayed home. She felt as if she had no one to identify with and felt so alone. And, clearly, she was totally done with me.

My mom wrote me cards with scriptures on them, but I didn't read them because they just made me mad. My prayer life was nonexistent. But God had other plans. It took a few months of living in that house alone to realize my anger had nothing to do with Hayley. I hit bottom like I did at college in Knoxville, but this time I was losing the love of my life. I was all alone and still miserable. What I thought would make it better didn't. The grass wasn't greener on the other side; it was the same as the piece of grass I was already standing on. I was low enough that I sought God, because

He was the only one who could pull me out of the mire. *What am I doing? What have I done? I love her!*

The Holy Spirit broke through, convicting me to make it work, to not quit my marriage. He let me know there was nothing that couldn't be worked out. Everything that we fought about was so little, so inconsequential. In that space and quiet, the Spirit broke a spot in my heart. (The rest of my heart would be broken years later!)

I think we tend to seek God's face when we're at our lowest lows. When we are on the mountaintops, we feel as though we need Him less. We have to have a balance. If I've learned anything, it's that when we are having the best of times, that's when we need to have our guard up the most because the next swing is coming and we have to be looking to duck Satan's blow. Satan attacks us when we're most vulnerable, which is often during those good times.

I realized, too, that I needed to make a stand and be my own person. My parents stayed on their knees about us, letting the Holy Spirit work, but they intentionally backed off from the situation after paying for and urging me to get counseling. I started calling Hayley. Would she come to counseling with me? She said to forget it. "Just give me those papers you've been working on," she said. She had shut me out. Who could blame her? Why would she want to rehash all the hurt? Go through it again? No way. She was done with me. So I would call her mom and ask how Hayley was doing. I knew I had been so wrong, and God was working on my heart. Her mom listened, angry with me at first, but then she knew something had changed. Those months were an especially hard time for her mom, with me talking her ear off and Hayley being miserably quiet. It was a dark time.

> The Holy Spirit broke through, convicting me to make it work, to not quit my marriage. He let me know there was nothing that couldn't be worked out.

Hayley prayed alone, so confused, so empty. Sometimes she didn't even know what to say to God. She was just sad. She knew He was there. Over time she felt a message from God: *Go back, and I will make this better than you can imagine*. About the same time, her dad sat her down, telling her she couldn't stay in this nowhere land anymore. He told her she had to go back to me and work it out or get a divorce. "Honey, you have to choose."

Hayley finally came to counseling with me, though her heart wasn't in it. She truly didn't want to be there, bringing all this hurt up again. She was only being obedient to what she'd felt from God, hoping for that promise. Four months after she moved out, she and the dog came home. Reluctantly.

5

Restoration and Renewed Hope

(Hayley)

Do not conform any longer to
the pattern of this world,
but be transformed by the renewing
of your mind. Then you will be able
to test and approve what
God's will is—his good,
pleasing and perfect will.

—

Romans 12:2

Nothing in me wanted to go back to Mike. I didn't even like him. It was all I could do to hang on to what God promised: *If you go back, I will make this better than you can imagine.* Mike was trying to be the gentleman I'd dated. But if he came near or tried to be sweet, I recoiled. I wasn't angry with Mike. I have never been one who can stay mad. I was deeply hurt. I felt I had been rejected. I had been my true self, gave my all, shared my world with Mike. These were things I had never done before, and when I finally allowed myself to share like that, I ended up rejected. I was broken and needed time heal. I could see Mike trying. There were times I wondered, *Who is this guy?* I needed to know I could trust him with my heart again.

In the beginning, during those stressful years, we had had no prayer time, no quiet, spiritual time together. God wasn't at the head of our marriage. He was a side thought on a Sunday. Mike was really seeking God and had started trying to study the Bible and grow his spiritual life. When I moved back in, we started to pray together. It wasn't the most comfortable thing to do, but I did it, though my guard was up.

One beautiful night I sat on the back porch. I had to get outside. I still couldn't stand being in the house with him. I thought, *Why am I here?* It was a clear night, full of bright stars and a full moon. "God! I can't do this," I prayed. "There's no way." The wind started to blow. But I knew it wasn't the wind. No trees moved; it was just on me. It was His Spirit. I breathed it in. Immediately I felt peace. A release. God hugged me. After that, my wall started coming down. Those feelings of cold disgust were gone. I didn't pull away when Mike tried to hug me. My heart slowly softened. I learned to trust God.

Through those dark eight months of our separation, Mike learned again how much he needed God. He couldn't make himself happy or expect something or someone in this world to bring him happiness. Mike had found his joy in God. Slowly we began to allow God to heal our marriage. We knew God needed to be the focus of our relationship. We had known these spiritual truths; we just never applied them. Think of a triangle. Mike and I are the points on the bottom. God is at the top. It's always work to keep God the focus of our marriage, but as we move closer to Him, we move closer together as a couple. His parents and mine never doubted. They knew God would knit us back together.

Then we met our lifesavers. God lined it up for us to get to know an incredible couple at church who shared their struggles and showed us a great example of marriage. I'm not exaggerating when I say they were a godsend. We learned that love is not a feeling. Love is a choice. Sometimes you have to choose to love someone even if you don't feel it at the time. Make the choice and the feeling will come later. Even when things are great, there will be moments when you don't feel love for someone, but you can't just walk out of your commitment. Choose to love them and love them well.

> Our marriage took daily work, and still does. We knew we were stronger for that struggle. We knew there was nothing we couldn't work through.

We continued for a while with counseling, which at first meant nothing to me because I didn't think I was learning anything new. But we kept going. We wanted help and were seeking God. Once we united on those two things, counseling and advice from this wise couple worked. There's nothing magical about counseling. If our hearts and intentions weren't right, counseling would have meant little. Both of us had felt alone and unheard, but through counseling we both received validation and were able to move forward.

There wasn't some amazing movie moment where we

fell back into each other's arms. But there came a time when I knew that darkness was behind us. We were reassured. Our marriage took daily work, and still does. We knew we were stronger for that struggle. We knew there was nothing we couldn't work through. We had a new confidence in ourselves as a couple and individually. Praying together is definitely the glue that binds us together and strengthens us. It allows us to hear each other's heart and needs, to be sensitive to them, and to encourage one another.

Obviously, our communication had been horrible. We had allowed little bitty snowballs in our lives to become great avalanches. We finally learned that God had to be first, and we also learned how to communicate and understand each other. We joke now that we have switched traditional roles in communication. Of the two of us, Mike's the talker. Sometimes he would say something just to say it out loud. He wasn't looking for a solution but wanted to hash something out. I wanted to solve the problem. If he stopped talking, I would follow him out to the barn or wherever and try to fix it. I mean, why would you tell me something if you don't want me to do something about it? I didn't understand that he just needed to vent and then have space.

During that time, we grew up. We're able to laugh at ourselves now (and often do). I'm so much more comfortable with who I am. And, yes, if I'm ticked about something, I'll say it. I learned to own what I think and feel. But I don't put a whole lot of weight on feelings, since they change like the wind. So now if Mike is upset about something, I don't react, but I give him five minutes. I recognize he's angry, but then let it go. Move on. He gets a little space, then we talk and move on. Molehills stay molehills, for the most part. We've learned to appreciate each other's strengths. Mike is a hard worker, always dependable, our protector, and a strong leader. Mike is the head of the home, and I am the heart.

We found the fun again in just being with each other. We bought a Harley and loved to take short trips on it on weekends. Those trips released the stresses of the work week and helped us escape and spend time together. We'd go riding through the country, to Georgia, to the Smoky Mountains, to Tennessee's Fall Creek Falls State Park, to anywhere we hadn't driven before. We loved that time spent on the bike together. Life before had been all about work and the struggle to pay the bills. We did nothing just for fun. The Harley was our fun. It was relaxing and freeing.

My parents could see a change in us, a sweetness, my mom calls it. I was comfortable in our relationship, in who I was. Now there's nothing we can't work through by just finding a way to communicate and to be understanding with each other.

We tried life without each other, and it didn't work. Now we have a deep confidence, a knowing, that we belong together. We're stuck with each other! Were we young and immature when we got married? Maybe, but our marriage was ordained by God. Our struggle was just part of it. Together, when we aim at Him, we can get through anything. He's in everything we do and in everything we are.

6

Starting a Family

(Hayley)

However, as it is written:
"No eye has seen, no ear has heard,
no mind has conceived
what God has prepared
for those who love him."

—

1 Corinthians 2:9

After God knitted our hearts back together, we knew we wanted to start a family. In God's timing, it took about seven months to conceive. I imagine God knew we weren't ready, so maybe that's why it took awhile.

After those months of hoping and disappointment, I conceived. At about four weeks along I knew I was pregnant. I'm sure most would think it was just wishful thinking again, being so positive that I was pregnant. Even though four or five home pregnancy tests came up negative, I told Mike that I knew I was pregnant; I could feel something inside. My doctor gave me a test with that knowing, "well, bless her heart" look. It was positive. *Well, I told you! Why were you so shocked?* Later, we found out it was a boy, although I knew in my heart that it was a boy before the ultrasound proved it at twenty weeks.

It would be a tough and scary pregnancy. After week twenty-four or so, I woke up one morning because somehow in my sleep I'd knocked a glass of water off the bedside table. The crash woke me up and I noticed I was bleeding profusely. Oh, God. I was losing the baby. We raced to the hospital. The nurse asked me to stand to get to the bed. I said, "No, I'm bleeding." She coaxed me up and started peeling off my clothes, which were soaked with blood. "You're bleeding!" she yelled at me. "Yes, I told you." Maybe I needed to act more frantic so people would have believed me.

They rushed me into an ambulance to go to a bigger hospital. It was serious and scary, but I still got excited about my first ambulance ride. I know it sounds silly, but it did make my heart beat fast as we raced down the interstate and through the streets of Nashville with lights flashing and siren blaring. I think even the EMT in the ambulance was amused by my excitement. He smiled as I tried to raise up my head and look out. Maybe it was my way to cope and stay calm. They wouldn't let Mike ride with me, so he raced behind us all the way to the hospital.

Ultrasounds showed the baby was fine, but my placenta was tearing away from my uterus. The placenta normally stays connected to the uterus until after the baby is born, but placental abruption causes hemorrhaging and can often mean a premature baby. On a magnesium drip and anti-contraction medicines, from then on I stayed on strict bed rest in the hospital. I wasn't allowed to wash my own hair, and every few days I was allowed to sit and take a shower while the nurse timed me. I hemorrhaged every five to seven days. "If you bleed another drop, we have to take the baby," I heard several times. I stayed on the borderline for about a month and a half as family rallied around and prayed.

I tried to read but couldn't focus because of the medicines, and words would look blurry after a while. I probably did hundreds of crossword puzzles to keep my mind busy throughout the long days lying in bed. Sometimes I would have to laugh at how hard it was for me to write, shaking so much that I couldn't read the letters I wrote. I slept a lot.

My mother, teacher friends, and church friends would come by or send goody baskets and flowers. I was so happy to see visitors. It made me think about one day being old in a nursing home and how much we long for conversation and to feel a part of the world.

I was scared. Mike was scared. The hand of God was all over this time, pulling Mike and me closer, unifying us. I so looked forward to Mike coming at night. A conversation! He would visit in the morning, go to work, and then come back in the evening.

We had a hard time choosing a name for our baby, but we knew one thing: his initials would be TD. Yes, touchdown. Finally, a few days before his birth, we chose Tyler Deacon. We both liked the name Tyler, and a deacon is a trusted leader in the church.

At thirty-two weeks, Mike was with me during one of what seemed like hundreds of ultrasounds. This one was different. The technician was visibly nervous and we asked what was wrong, but she wasn't allowed to tell us what she saw. "Your doctor will be coming quickly," she said. We think she must have seen my placenta torn from the uterus. About three hours later, the doctor on call checked me and said I could wait to deliver. The nurses knew better and worried and checked on me. That doctor came back at about 9:00 p.m. and announced he'd done three C-sections that day and was going to bed. He said that I would be okay until the morning, when he'd come back to do my C-section. We thought, *Are you kidding me?* but didn't fight what the doctor said. A few hours later, I hemorrhaged and blood was everywhere, dripping off the bed. I was in and out of consciousness and blacking out from pain.

Mike was with me during one of what seemed like hundreds of ultrasounds. This one was different. The technician was visibly nervous and we asked what was wrong, but she wasn't allowed to tell us.

They rushed me out of my room and into another. I don't know why, but I think they moved my plants with me. Weird detail to remember, I know. As out of it as I was, I opened my eyes, saw the plants, and thought, *I'm dead. This is the funeral home.* Everything happened so fast, in such a confusing way. Poor Mike was stuck out in the hallway alone because he wasn't allowed in with me. As they rubbed on my belly and prepped me for surgery, I saw surgical tools, and in my odd state of mind, I kept trying to tell them, "I'm not asleep yet. I'm not asleep yet." They tried to hold me down and put a mask on me. I heard voices, "Get started now. He's not here. We have to do this now."

At about 1:00 a.m., our sweet Tyler Deacon was born on September 30, 2004, a month and half early. Weighing four pounds, he was whisked off to the neonatal intensive care unit. The doctor found Mike in the hall and told him I'd lost a lot of blood. *No kidding*, he said to himself. "It's really touchy," he said. "We'll have to see how she does overnight." *Whaaaat? What are you saying*? They were telling him I might not make it. Mike chokes up now remembering that helpless feeling. I was in the trauma unit, so he couldn't see me. Of course, he'd called family, who all arrived throughout that morning.

He followed Tyler to the NICU, which let him have something else to focus on while they worked to stabilize me. He remembers praying and trusting God that it was all going to work out. He had a confidence in Christ and peace that He had this under control. He remembers thinking, *My goodness, we were already at the hospital for the last six weeks, so we couldn't have been in any better place. How could God not have this? He placed us here.*

The next morning, miraculously, I was stable enough

to be moved back to my regular room. Those first few days were a blur. I knew nothing about how close to death I had come. Apparently my face was white as snow or, I guess, pale as death. I'd had two transfusions, but for some reason couldn't have more. I woke up to nurses pushing on my uterus, the usual practice after a birth. I think I screamed, but no sound came out. As I woke up from my fog days later, I remember saying in a lightheaded wonder, "I have a baby!" And my mom said, "Yes, you *do* have a baby." Then I was out of it again. Nurses I didn't know were visiting just to see me. Alive.

A nurse pulled Mike aside a day after Tyler was born and told him that I was lucky to be alive, much less our son. She had never seen it that bad. She'd never seen someone lose that much blood . . . and survive. Another doctor spoke to Mike later telling him not to worry about any bills. We never received a bill, a claim, or anything for all of my six weeks in the hospital, the birth, or Tyler's stay in the NICU.

Finally, they wheeled me in to visit Tyler. I was so wobbly as I stood next to his preemie box. I could touch him, but I so wanted to hold his precious little body. I couldn't nurse him since he was fed through a tube, so I pumped. I went home after a week, but we had to leave tiny Tyler. He couldn't breathe well or suck or regulate his body temperature. I would cry every night having to leave him there in the NICU. I couldn't stand it. It was like leaving my arms there. He was a part of me.

When I was in the hospital, Mike would ride there on our Harley we used to enjoy riding together. It was cheap on fuel and a stress reliever for him. After Tyler came home, we sold the Harley. Having a child changes priorities, and he worried about riding it. Mostly he worried about other drivers on the road. Knowing God gives us each breath we have every time we inhale, he felt he wasn't being responsible if he continued to ride. And Tyler and I couldn't ride on it with him, so that season was over. We later used the money for a down payment on our house.

Six weeks after Tyler's birth, we brought our now-healthy boy home, appropriately just a few weeks before Thanksgiving. It was a perfect, sweet time with the cutest baby in entire world. Life was wonderful. I was living on adrenalin because physically I was still fairly weak. Since I couldn't walk well upstairs to his room, he slept in a bassinet next to our bed.

Tyler was a few months old when we found our house and moved off Mike's parents' farm. Still very near his family, the house was a great deal but needed a lot of work. Our family helped us with flooring, paint, and other things to make it the perfect place for our little family. This is when I became a little obsessive about keeping the house clean for our preemie, making sure the floors were spotless, the tables disinfected. Mike worked hard, long hours to make the horse barn successful. He laments those lost baby-toddler years, gone in a blink.

I enjoyed every moment at home with Tyler. The following February, in 2005, I went back to teaching kindergarten. I absolutely love teaching, but leaving Tyler was heart wrenching. My job had the health insurance, and we needed the money. All I could think was, *I am supposed to be home with my baby*. I fought back tears every day when I dropped off Tyler at day care those first months. And that was even with him being cared for in a nursery at my school that was one door down the hall. No, I didn't even like that. Someone else was holding him. What if he did something extraordinary and I missed it? My mom laughs with me now that I used to worry about scarring him for life when I left him with her for a few hours to run errands. The in-school nursery program ended the next year and we found other care, but eventually he stayed with Mike's mom, Cathy Jones. She's forever dubbed "Yay Yay," which was baby Tyler's

> I was alone in my classroom when I heard a man's voice say, "You will have a baby." I went out to the hallway looking for the man. Nobody was there but me. I knew the voice was God's.

attempt at "C. J.," which she wanted to be called. It stuck.

The seed to adopt a child had stayed planted in the backs of our minds. And after all the scares having Tyler, we didn't know what another pregnancy would bring. If I got stuck in the hospital again, who would take care of Tyler? As mentioned earlier, our brief exploration into adopting from Ethiopia hadn't felt right, so we had abandoned the pursuit for the time being. The paperwork had sat on the kitchen counter and eventually was shuffled into a drawer.

From 2001 to 2008, Mike and his dad put everything they had into making their equestrian center successful. But the recession made it even tougher. Mike and his dad made the gut-wrenching decision to close the barn in March 2008. It was a loss we all felt. Thankfully, the general manager at Milcrofton Utility District had visited the farm just as they were about to have a family meeting about closing it. It led to a talk about job openings, and he said he was looking for an assistant to train. Mike interviewed and started the next month as assistant general manager. Mike does everything 110 percent and dove in to learn everything he could about his new profession. Though it was a pay cut, he saw the job as full of opportunity and promise.

At about the same time Mike changed jobs, on a day that a few of us teachers had prayed together before school, I sat during a planning period putting away my color-coded files for the week. I was alone in my classroom when I heard a man's voice say, "You will have a baby." I went out to the hallway looking for the man. No one was there. I checked the cubby room and the next classroom. Nobody was there but me. I knew the voice was God's.

I texted Mike, "I just heard God tell me I'm going to have a baby." He texted back, "Well, I guess we can start practicing." That's my Mike, always willing to do God's will. On our first try, I became pregnant. Again, I knew it before I should have. The home pregnancy test was negative; a test at the doctor's office was negative. I had an ultrasound. No, they said, I wasn't pregnant; it was a cyst. Again, I felt the "bless her heart" attitude toward me. A cyst? No, I knew I was pregnant.

A few weeks went by and I'd missed another period. So I bought another pregnancy test and, finally, this one was positive. I told my shocked doctor, and the ultrasound confirmed it. But based on my history, they were concerned. "Let's see how far it gets," she said. They had fears, but I didn't. God had clearly said I would have a baby. I told Mike everything would be fine.

I did end up on bed rest at home because of early contractions, but this pregnancy was much easier. Still, at thirty-four weeks, something wasn't right. The baby was going to have to be delivered by emergency C-section after I started losing fluid. I told every nurse and doctor in contact with me, "I'm seeing this one! Don't you dare knock me out.

I'm witnessing this one." This time I had a spinal block, and Mike stayed by my head during the delivery.

Our five-pound Tucker Derby (yes, TD!) was born February 2, 2009. I was so shocked and thrilled when they wheeled him into my room because I'd geared myself up to expect another time in NICU. I nursed him and had a good, normal two days at the hospital. That pregnancy was another spiritual turning point for me. I don't want to do anything if God's not telling me to do it.

After maternity leave, I taught my sweet kindergartners for the last five or six weeks of school. This time there were no tears, but I still deeply felt the heart tug to be home. I wanted to be the one who laughed with them when they played and bounced them on my hip all around the house when they were fussy. When they played outside on the swing, I wanted to be the one pushing them, singing to them. When they smeared their lunch all over their faces . . . and on the wall and floor . . . I wanted to be the one who held those memories. Life goes by so quickly, and I want all the memories I can get. To me, these are the joys in life, the treasures.

Work was a really touchy subject with Mike, because while he would have loved it if I could stay home, we just couldn't afford it. But I knew this wasn't what I was supposed to be doing. If I brought it up, the discussion ended quickly because the money didn't add up.

I read Bible stories to Ty each night. We would curl up in his bed and read until I was almost asleep. He would listen intently, and we would talk about what he was thinking and feeling as I would scratch his back. I would sing my favorite hymns to Tucker while rocking him to sleep at naptime and at night. He would stare into my eyes and reach for my face. The memories of his fat, little fingers and his soft, sweet lips still linger in my mind.

I'd pray those nights I was awake with baby Tucker, just begging God, *What can I do? I know I'm supposed to be here.* Every mother does it differently, but for me, I was supposed to be home. This was my role as a mother, and I couldn't do it. I was so happy that Yay Yay could care for them while we were at work, but I was missing this precious time with my boys.

One day I was cleaning the guest room and flopped down on the bed in desperate prayer. *Oh, God, what should I do to show Mike I'm supposed to be home?* I've heard the audible voice of God twice in my life. The first time He told me I would have a baby. This time, as I lay on the bed, I heard Him say, "This is not your problem, it's Mine." I shot straight up. *Yes!* I giggled to myself. *Yes, it is* Your *problem. Not mine.* Peace washed over me. He had a plan and would work it out. So many things are just not our problems; they're His. I stopped owning the work dilemma and gave the burden to Him. God will say exactly the words we need, in the way we need to hear them. Those few words were all I needed.

A few weeks later, it was Mike who brought up the work conversation. "Hayley, what do you think about working part-time?" Oh yes! That was the perfect step forward. Mike's job had health insurance, and he was making quick progress through a five-year training plan to become general manager. The next school year, in fall 2009, I would share my job with another teacher. God had worked. He moved all the pieces of our life to make room for His next miracle.

7

Think Big!

(Mike)

We can make our plans,

but the LORD determines our steps.

—

Proverbs 16:9 NLT

Yes, God set up all the details of our life. When Tyler was a baby, I had worked holidays and all hours of the night to meet customers or check on sick horses. I missed so much family life because I was consumed with our equestrian center business. My job change allowed me to be home after 4:00 p.m. as long as there wasn't a water leak or any other after-hours emergency. I could turn work off and go home to enjoy my family. We actually had dinner together and family time we hadn't had before. I made sure I soaked up Tucker's babyhood and tried to grow my relationship with Tyler. I loved reading books together and getting down on the floor to play with them.

Spiritually, we felt an itch. Church had become comfortable. I was a deacon at our church for a couple of years. We found a smaller congregation and worshipped there for a while, then eventually went back to the bigger church. We stayed involved with our Sunday school class friends and were busy with the boys. We both felt a yearning, a hole, a something's-missing urge.

God was really pulling on us, and we knew we were

gearing up for something but just weren't sure what. Like we've said, we'd thought about ways to adopt, but since nothing had felt right about it yet, we really didn't know what God was planning. We didn't talk about it a lot, but God worked on us privately. Hayley taught part-time, which was perfect. Our budget still worked on paper, and she could spend a lot of time with our boys.

Hayley. I can't say enough about this saint. She is often the closest thing I have to Jesus. God really knew what He was doing when He gave me her. It's all in His perfect plan for our lives. Along with God, she makes me whole! She exhibits all the fruits of the Spirit: love, joy, peace, patience, kindness, goodness, faithfulness, gentleness, and self-control. I truly am the luckiest guy alive to have her by my side.

> We both felt a yearning, a hole, a something's-missing urge. God was really pulling on us, and we knew we were gearing up for something but just weren't sure what.

In 2010, after Hayley met with Erica and we prayed over our role in Sierra Leone, the hole started to fill. This was it. We would adopt there. Our childhood dreams about mission work and adoption were finally coming true, and it all made sense. Seeking God's face and His will for us was our focus during this time. We knew God was calling us to think bigger.

Initially we had no idea, though, what "bigger" might mean. As I grabbed my Father's knees in prayer that night on the bedroom floor, crying out to Him, I was forever changed. God broke me. He was calling us to adopt those eight children whom He had chosen for us. God had been working on me for years, but now I heard Him and trusted in a way I had never trusted before. It took all those learning curves over the years to get us to the place where we were spiritually filled and ready to be vessels and do whatever He called us to. God the Provider, God Almighty, the One who would provide everything we would need, including the words to tell the world about what we were planning to do.

My planning and budgeting to adopt eight children? Out the window. I didn't worry about it anymore. God had it. I'd worry at times when I got bogged down and my human nature would take over, but I didn't let it last long because I knew it was Satan attacking me, and I didn't want to give in or be consumed. We would get to points along the way when money was about to dry up, and *bam*, God would provide in His perfect timing. He's done that all along. God is so good!

I stayed quiet for a few days after that life-changing prayer on our bedroom floor. I couldn't talk to anyone about it because I would probably start crying. One day I got to the shop early before work started to talk with about ten of my guys. I didn't go into the whole prayer, but told them we were going to adopt and that God had touched our hearts. I shared with them about the eight. And there I was, crying like a baby in front of my field crew.

A couple of the guys stuffed their hands in their pockets, said, "Hmm," and walked away. And a few of them patted me on the back. They didn't know what to say. They responded probably like I would have before that prayer changed me. I share the tears pretty easily now with the world. Ask me today and I still choke up reliving that prayer. After I talked to the guys, I told the office workers, who were mostly women. One of them, a churchgoer, flat out told me, "Y'all are nuts." She would be the first but definitely not the last to tell us that.

8

Sharing Our Dream with the World

(Hayley)

Have I not commanded you?
Be strong and courageous.
Do not be terrified;
do not be discouraged,
for the LORD *your God*
will be with you wherever you go.

—

Joshua 1:9

We both slept soundly the night God made it clear to Mike that we should adopt these eight children, knowing that He had this and He could do anything. We could take on the world. And then I woke up.

I've never been one to share deep things with people. If I'm going through something, I usually don't talk about it but would rather just push through and do it. After it's over, I can look back and talk about it. I'm very outgoing, but the deep, potentially scary stuff seems safer inside. Mom says I might not express everything, but from a young age I felt everything deeply. She remembers a time sitting on the curb with me as I looked up at the stars, being contemplative. I would worry when she left to run an errand that she wouldn't come back. As a teen, I got quieter, not even telling her about the hard social time I had after I skipped a grade.

Our decision about adopting eight children wasn't based on a feeling exactly, but a *knowing*. It was, however, something big, something deep that we could not keep to ourselves. And that, in itself, was enough to freak me out. But who would we tell first? Erica Stone, of course.

Monday morning, on one of my days off, after my prayer warrior left for work and Tyler went to kindergarten, it was just me and baby Tucker at home. I wasn't sure how to tell Erica. I could call, but then I didn't know if I would have the words to explain. Texting wouldn't work. I decided e-mail was the safest way. Throughout that morning, after I wrote that we wanted "the eight," I left the message sitting on my computer. I came back and reread it, rewrote it, and with my stomach in knots I finally hit send.

> I held the computer in my lap, and our hearts beat fast as we met our family. As each picture filled the screen, we yelled, "It's a boy!" Then "It's a boy!" and yet again, "It's a boy!"

Erica read it about three times. She had her husband, Jason, look at it to make sure she had read it correctly. Then she called me. All my dread turned into joy. I was expecting those practical questions, and had even written about how we could make room downstairs. Justifying it. Explaining our decision. But Erica, bless her soul, didn't need that kind of explanation. She just got it. Over the next three years, she and I would become so close. We would walk this road together, sometimes sprinting, sometimes holding each other up. After talking to her that morning, I was on top of the world again.

Remember, we knew absolutely nothing about these children. Ages? Genders? Needs? Nothing. All we knew was there were eight of them. Mike and I tossed around possibilities that morning before he left for work. "What if it's eight girls?" I said. "Oh my gosh, I can't do eight girls." When my sister and I were young, I'd wanted a brother, and I had always pictured myself as a mom of boys. But we decided, "It is what it is. We know we're adopting these children, so the details are just details." When Erica told me it was seven boys and one girl, I had to laugh. This was totally chosen and made for us. It couldn't have been more perfect. Again, another God move.

Erica e-mailed us photos of the children. I'll never forget sitting on the couch with Mike and Tyler, opening these huge files. Tyler, then four, had been part of our prayers, asking God what His plan was for our family. Tyler was so excited at the thought of more brothers or sisters, but mostly he was hoping to have a playmate his age. He beamed with excitement.

I held the computer in my lap, and our hearts beat fast as we met our family. We'd click on each photo, and it would start loading at the top of the screen and open ever so slowly. As each picture filled the screen, we yelled, "It's a boy!" Then "It's a boy!" and yet again, "It's a boy!"

We pored over these photos, knowing they were God's gift to us, and guessed at their ages, knowing we were probably wrong. (We were.) Seeing their pictures for the first time made it all so precious, so exciting, so real. We printed wallet-sized versions, and I carried them from then on. Anytime someone asked about the adoption, I'd pull those pictures out of my purse just like any proud parent. People could identify with photos, so that's how we introduced them from day one. I clung to those photos.

We knew these were our children, but would our parents understand? Oh, my stomach. I was anxious to tell both sets of parents, but I desperately needed my own parents, Bill and Susan Drake, to be on board with our decision. On Father's Day 2010, we had Mike's parents, Ken and Cathy Jones, over in the afternoon and my parents that night. We knew we were doing the right thing, but I felt like I had to prove it. God had told us clearly what was going to happen. He certainly didn't need me to prove anything for Him, but I was completely nervous about what my parents would say and how I could possibly explain. My biggest fear was the "how" question. We just didn't have answers to all the practical questions.

Our parents had known for years that we wanted to adopt since we'd talked about it many times. We explained that we'd looked at Ethiopia and South Africa, but just never felt peaceful about those places. We told my parents that we'd really been praying about it, and that Sierra Leone would be the country. "We found a sibling group," I said nervously.

"A group? What do you mean, *a group*?" my dad asked.

I showed one photo, then another, then another as I handed them to my mom. "Eight. A sibling group of eight," I said as she stared at me with all eight photos in her hands. More knots in my stomach. It was like torture to have to explain everything.

"I could see your mouth moving after that," my mom remembers. "But I couldn't hear anything you were saying. I couldn't process that many children."

I knew it was overwhelming for them. I so wanted them to understand and to see it the way we did.

"I got what you were saying spiritually, but I still had this cloud on me," my mom says. "I couldn't process how you would be able to take care of ten children." But they never doubted this was from God. They could just tell. My dad, always even-keeled, was quiet but smiled. My mom, who had just recently buried her father and learned my sister, Courtney, and her husband, Joey, were going to South Africa to be missionaries, was shell-shocked. She believed and knew our conviction was sincere and true, but she worried. What mother wouldn't worry after her daughter announced something like that?

"How?" she asked.

"I don't know," I told her. "But I know I'm supposed to do it."

For the logical, thinking person, there were issues.

Money, the size of our house. Oh, right, did I mention money? After this talk with my parents, I'm sure they had no doubt something had happened to their little girl. "You can ask me how it will all work again tomorrow and I'm still not going to know, and you're going to have to be okay with it," I would say more than once when Mom asked a perfectly logical question. Or, "I don't know how. But God knows." They had been at our house years ago, when I was crying and upset because we hadn't set up college funds yet for Tyler and Tucker. They'd seen us struggle to make ends meet. But we hugged and cried. Despite their concerns, they immediately supported us. I can just imagine their conversation on the drive home.

Later that same day, Mike's parents cried as he cried telling them about his prayer. Was this their same tough boy who would break horses, break tackles, and never cry? Cathy and Ken's loving, immediate reaction floored us. They were ready to do whatever they could to help. God's timing of this was poignant. This was the middle of the recession, and they had closed the horse farm and suffered great financial loss. At that point, they were getting back on their feet, so right then I think they needed this in their lives. It gave focus and shaped everyone for the future. The more Mike talked, the more he broke down. They had never seen him emotional like that. It was so obvious something had happened to him. He was broken. This wasn't just an idea. This was God.

"If God has told you to do this, then do it, and He will help you do it," Cathy told us.

Most people in our lives believed faith in God was safe, structured. Faith wasn't crazy. This was their introduction to crazy, radical obedience. I can't speak for all Baptist churches, but growing up there, I remember learning about the Holy Spirit that lived during Bible days. It never seemed like something that would pertain to my life now. It was after my first trip to meet the children that we told people at church that God spoke to us, that He told us to do this. Some got it but, well, many didn't. We would sometimes feel like outsiders even at our church. I guess anyone on an unfamiliar journey would feel that isolation. If someone else hasn't been through it and can't identify, your new journey sets you apart.

> Most people in our lives believed faith in God was safe, structured. Faith wasn't crazy. This was their introduction to crazy, radical obedience.

We decided to tell Mike's grandparents about a week later. And nerves hit me again. They had grown up in a different time, and even though they were churchgoers, races didn't mix much, let alone live in the same house. I'll never forget telling Beatrice Jones, Mike's grandma. When he was young, Mike remembers Granny saying "negroes" and the grandkids trying to correct her, "No, Granny, it's African-Americans."

He also remembers as a small boy one hot summer day giving water to the guys working for the local power company. Granny Jones served it in glasses to the white men but in paper cups to the two black men on the crew. When he asked why the black men didn't get glasses, she said, "You can't clean those cups honey. You got to just throw them away."

We weren't expecting great reactions from his grandparents. We didn't think they'd understand. We were wrong.

Granny Jones, who was mostly blind by then, sat at the table at Mike's brother Brian's house. She could only see a little pinhole of light out of one eye after a stroke and surgery and would turn her head to try to see us. We told her what God had put on our hearts. We would adopt eight children from Sierra Leone. Tears ran down her cheeks. She kept patting our hands and saying how proud she was. Although she couldn't see physically, the Lord opened the eyes of her heart that day to see beyond the prejudices and ignorance of her generation and helped her to love all people as children of God, regardless of their skin color.

Granny talked about how she wanted to help, but she was a widow and said she didn't have a lot of money and couldn't work. She broke my heart.

"We don't need you to do anything," we told her. "Just pray."

That wonderful lady ended up selling a burial plot to buy what she wanted to get them. Each child got a towel, a washcloth, bed sheets, and blankets. Mike's mom did the shopping, but Granny Jones told her to get pink for our girl and had certain colors in mind for the boys. She told all of her friends at her assisted-living home about the adoption, displayed their photos there, and prayed for them.

Mike's maternal grandparents were just as thrilled. Rev. William and Catherine Cox, also known as Paw Paw and Granny Cox, loved our news and wanted to help. Their words echoed Cathy's: "If God told you, then do it." They had spent their life together traveling and serving the ministry through their music. Granny played the organ and Paw Paw sang. They were amazed at what God was doing in our life. Their small church rallied behind us in prayer and support. I couldn't believe it. It was just God. Within a month of our revelation, our whole family was on board.

9

Our Great Eight's Story

(Hayley)

Give thanks to the Lord,
for he is good; his love endures forever.
Let the redeemed of the LORD *say this—*
those he redeemed from
the hand of the foe.

—

Psalm 107:1–2

Our children grew up in one of the world's poorest countries, where 70 percent of its people live below the poverty line (NationsEncyclopedia.com). Ironically, it also has beautiful beaches, lovely mountains, and diverse resources such as diamonds, gold, rutile, and bauxite. A decade of civil war left deep scars. The United Nations lists Sierra Leone as one of the world's "least livable" countries, based on its poverty and poor quality of life (Human Development Index by the United Nations Development Programme). The 2014 Ebola epidemic just added insult to injury. I can't imagine how this country will cope long term. We have loved ones there, family. We prayed for protection over Shenge, our children's village, as this virus ravaged the country.

Our children survived poverty, the loss of their father, and eventually their mother being unable to take care of them. But God took tragedy and turned it into something beautiful. Their life stories can help them become world changers. But their stories are just that—theirs. They are children. They accept that their stories are different from others and know God will use them, but there are times when they don't want to be known as "that kid that went through that" or "that kid who did that." Sometimes they just want to be "normal." Beyond what they wanted us to write about in this book, each of our children will make choices regarding what parts of their lives to share and with whom to share them when they are old enough, just like each one of us does. As their parents, we will protect them and respect that right.

The children like to ask Michael questions about the village and want him to tell stories of when they were little. We laugh a lot and enjoy these stories so much.

Michael, our oldest, is our storyteller. He remembers his young life in Shenge and helps his brothers and sister remember theirs. Our youngest, Zion, was only two years old when they went to live at The Raining Season center. The children like to ask Michael questions about the village and want him to tell stories of when they were little. We laugh a lot and enjoy these stories so much. It is these happy memories that we treasure and want to share now.

Shenge lays along the Atlantic Ocean about a five- or six-hour bumpy ride south of the capital city of Freetown in Sierra Leone. English is the country's official language, but Krio is widely spoken and Shenge villagers speak Sherbro.

It's a village filled with fishermen and rice farmers, where families are large. My children's house held at least a dozen people including grandparents. Shenge will always have a part of my heart. The orange dirt, the palm trees with big coconuts, the clay houses with thatched roofs, the people walking up and down the dirt roads carrying their goods on their heads or fetching water in giant jugs . . . My soul feels peace there. I cannot explain the feeling, but I love that place. It is the home of our extended family.

Life is simple, but don't confuse that with easy. Life is anything but easy. Everyone stays busy in order to survive. Our children's family makes their living as rice farmers. Every morning families walk to their rice farms to work. The farm is a few acres of the bush a family has bought to grow rice for one season. "If you have luck, you could buy it again for the next season if someone doesn't buy it before you," Michael says.

To prepare the rice field, they clear it with a machete-like knife with a homemade wooden handle. They walk through the acres chopping down trees and cutting all the grasses. Once the field is all cut by hand, it must dry. Then they burn the leaves and grasses that were left in the field, scatter the rice in sections, and hoe it to cover the seeds. While the rice is growing, the children must go every day to chase birds away and weed the acres. At harvest, they cut the rice with that machete-like knife and bundle it together with the leftover stems. They carry the bundles on their heads all the way back to their house. The work is hard. The days are long. There are no machines or tractors to help.

In the village, there is a "school." During planting season, the schoolchildren hike three hours to their teacher's bush-land to plant his rice field. Medical care is available if mission trips have reached out that far. There are no cars in the village, but there are some ocadas, which are like dirt bikes.

Heat and humidity are constant, with the mean temperature at eighty-one degrees. Two distinct seasons govern the subsistence life, the dry season from November to April, and the wet season the rest of the year. The heaviest rains hit in July, August, and September. A rainstorm there isn't like rain here. Storms come hard and wash away bridges, buildings, and people. Freetown gets an average of 144 inches of rain each year.

Food is whatever villagers can grow, catch, or hunt. The bush is full of animals like monkeys, bush rats, bush pigs, squirrels, deer, and something my children call a "cutting grass," which is somewhat like a beaver. All of these animals make a great meal when you are hungry. When I say hunt animals, I don't mean they sit in tree stand and shoot them with a gun. They make traps from sticks and grasses and catch them by hand. Or, if a villager is lucky, he might have a dog. Michael had a dog named Lasinia, which means "what you don't know don't talk about it" in Sherbro. Lasinia would bark and chase the animals, and Michael would sprint behind him.

Once Lasinia killed and dropped the animal, Michael would have a meal. If the bush animal wasn't dead yet, Michael would finish it off. He would fry it up on the fire in the "kitchen." The outside kitchen was what we would call a campfire with tall sticks on four sides and grasses making a roof. Meals always include rice, sometimes seafood or goat. There are no set meal times. You eat when you have something to eat. If not, you might not eat at all. The villagers are incredibly creative and can make the best out of very little.

Fruit grows in the bush too. Mangoes, guava, and plantains. Nothing is as good as plantain fried over an open fire. Bananas, pineapples, oranges, papayas, and coconuts can be grown there. Michael and some of the boys in the village would climb high in the coconut trees and take the coconuts. They would hide them under their shirts if they were wearing one. I laugh at the thought of this . . . Did they really think no one would notice them? He remembers the tree bark was so rough that it left scars on his chest.

Once the rice is harvested, villagers travel into town, often by ferry, to sell it. In September 2009, villagers loaded up their goods on a ferry bound for Freetown. The boat carried hundreds of villagers. It capsized and almost everyone died in one of Sierra Leone's worst ferry tragedies. Despite living near the coast, most people don't know how to swim because water is a very fearful thing there. That day changed everything for many families, including our children's. They lost their father, aunts, an uncle, cousins, friends. They lost so much that day. Michael remembers. The news came at night and the children were awoken. The story goes that one of the few survivors swam to safety and got word out that the boat had capsized and that most were killed. They had hope for more survivors until the boat's manifest was released.

Hundreds of men from Shenge died, devastating the village. The villagers gathered, and my children remember the wailing, the heartbreak, the sadness that overtook their village as the news spread. The mourning time was short because life is hard and work still has to be done. Survival became the fuel that kept the living going. They had to move on, get past the tragedy, and focus on trying to live. Villagers are very dependent on each other and operate in groups. There is no personal business; everything is dealt with together.

My children's lives were forever altered by the loss of their father, the man who led them. There were days the children didn't eat. The women still worked the rice farm, but they had to prepare meals, which take a long time. They were very limited in how much money they could make because they couldn't spend all day in the fields working;

they had mouths to feed. For almost a year, villagers coped and helped each other, but there was only so much they could do. The kids were starving. Food was scarce, so scarce that one child ate dirt.

Staff at The Raining Season, which had opened its orphan care center earlier in 2009, got word about the suffering children in Shenge. They went out to meet with families a few times and brought the neediest children, including ours, to the center. It's hard to explain how a family can let children go to live with someone else. It's a different world. It's survival. They knew The Raining Season would care for the children.

> That day changed everything for many families, including our children's. They lost their father, aunts, an uncle, cousins, friends. They lost so much that day.

The children remember the rough journey to Freetown on their first ride in an automobile in a black poda, which is like a van with rows of metal benches that are not made for comfort. The staff gave them bread and water before the long road trip. But their first taste of bread did not settle well in their stomachs on the bumpy dirt roads. Several of them vomited all over themselves and the poda. It was hot, smelly, and scary as they left the only home they had ever known.

Suffering, loss, heartbreak . . . but God still was with them. And He already had a plan for redemption, joy, and healing. At The Raining Season, they ate, they had beds, and they went to school and started to learn English and Krio, which is spoken in Freetown. They began studying the Bible and learning about Jesus. It is here where I would meet them about six months later. Here, where God would begin unfolding a new chapter in their lives. Broken, but not destroyed . . . there would be light at the end of the tunnel.

I got to meet some of the members of their birth family when they visited the center. We took photos, and staff told their family in Sherbro that I was sponsoring and taking care of the kids. They got to see photos of Mike and the boys, and they seemed happy and relieved. The children were safe and fed. It's such a different, survival-based mind-set in Sierra Leone that it's hard for Americans to really ever understand. A few months after the children left the village, their family signed over parental rights to TRS.

As the oldest boy, I think Michael had always been a father figure for his siblings. He exudes a calm authority and gentleness so he sets the tone for all the younger ones. He is delightful. He had such a hard life, but he is full of joy.

Our children would spend three years at the orphanage. Those years, as arduous as they were, gave the children time to heal and process things. Those first few days here at home, Michael told Mike and me so many stories. Maybe it was cathartic for him. We've talked about places he wants to show me like the coconut trees he'd climb or the field he'd cut through when he was running to school. Now he wonders how he can help his village. They have dreams like all other kids. Most of them want to be famous soccer players. Michael dreams of using his gifts, talents, and money to help other children. He believes in adoption and what it does for children. He knows what it is like to be with and without. He drew out a complex idea to build a children's center, which has separate places for boys and for girls. He wants a large center area with a roof but open sides where the children can play soccer or other games. He has thoughts about what type of people would work with the children and ways the center could benefit the community. He definitely has a heart for others.

They all pray for God's mercy on their village and want to share Jesus with them. My world changers.

10

When One Door Closes, Bang on Another

(Hayley)

Remember how the L*ORD* *your God led you all the way in the desert these forty years, to humble you and to test you in order to know what was in your heart, whether or not you would keep his commands.*

—

Deuteronomy 8:2

Our resolve and peace after Mike's prayer stayed intact throughout the summer 2010 as we prepared for my first trip to Sierra Leone to meet the children face to face that fall. God had showed us our children—all we had to do was get them home! But writing this part of our story means digging back into pain and despair. I've hidden it deep, even from myself. It makes me want to give up trying to write it now. How can I really put this part of the journey into words? Three years of emotion, challenges, heartache, brokenness, and injustice. Words don't seem to touch this pain. How do I describe this adequately? And though my children are free from the oppression there, others whom we love are not yet.

I carried the children's photos in my purse everywhere I went. I had stared at them, looking in their eyes, at their features. But I wanted to touch them, learn their mannerisms, hear their voices, their accents, their laughter. It would be my first trip out of the country since childhood. I needed a passport, a visa, several vaccinations, a plane ticket, and to prepare myself and my two boys for my absence for the first time in their lives. I was teaching part time, so I had more leeway to ask for time off. I would take this mission trip with Erica and six others as Mike had only one week of vacation a year and we weren't sure what was next. We knew Erica's adoption had taken years, but we understood the country would be more open now.

We jumped off the cliff headfirst into a sea of unknowns. Unlike many international adoptions, we weren't waiting for a child referral from an agency. We had no agency. This was a completely independent adoption. The Raining Season was set up to care for orphans. It's not an adoption agency. First, we needed financial approval from U.S. Immigration and a home study. We wanted both of those complete to take with me on my trip in September. If I had all of that together, maybe I could get the adoption through court. Throughout the journey, certain Bible verses sustained me. Early on, it was Jeremiah 29:11: "'For I know the plans I have for you,' declares the LORD, 'plans to prosper you and not to harm you, plans to give you hope and a future.'"

According to the federal formula, our income was just above the cutoff for the number of children we wanted to adopt. It was enough. We filled out the paperwork, got fingerprinted, and waited for approval. Whatever it took, we were willing to do it. We had to send in some extra information, but we were approved. Praise God for the first step. For our home study, we took the classes, met with all necessary people, and met again. We explained our story. We weren't randomly wanting to adopt eight children. In fact, it was not our idea at all; it was God's. Some people got it, and some did not. Because of the unusually large number, we met with someone higher up, who told us she was putting her job on the line for this. We had barely made financial approval, and she really didn't know us at the time. She had to trust us. Since then, she's actually traveled there and has worked with The Raining Season.

All these preparatory steps would have to work out because this adoption was already God-approved. We had a deep knowing about the big picture, but the unknowns still cluttered our minds. Outside of family, only a few people at church knew what we were embarking upon.

We sponsored all eight children immediately, and that provided food, medical care, education, and clothing, and helped pay staff at The Raining Season. We couldn't afford forty dollars per child each month, but the center worked with us, and we would give as much as we could. Then we focused on saving for known and unknown expenses to come such as airfare for trips, attorneys there, our home study, and the biggest expense, remodeling our four-bedroom house. We weren't sure how this was all going to get done, and we knew we couldn't get started without help. We shared our story in several Sunday school classes, many of which would come alongside us.

I'll never forget another sweet moment of God speaking through others into our calling. I was pushing Tucker on our playset's swing and was on the phone with Erica. During one of her mission trips, one of the women with her had been impacted by sweet Kadiatu, then just eight years old. She worried about this little girl and prayed with Erica for her. They knew her chances for adoption were dismal because she was part of a huge sibling group. They prayed and God heard. It's been our running joke ever since that it's all Erica's fault. She prayed and it happened. God would take care of Kadiatu.

As Mike and I lay in bed and prayed together every night, I asked God to give me faith that is immeasurable and immovable. Every night I prayed for this. Be careful what you ask for! You know when you ask God for some kind of quality like faith or patience, you won't just wake up with it. No, instead He will give you every opportunity to learn and practice your requested quality. So yes, God did answer my prayer. Every. Day. He answered it by giving me another day to exercise faith in Him to bring about what He had called us to do. If you ask my children my favorite verse, they'll tell you it's Hebrews 11:1: "Now faith is being sure of

I asked God to give me faith that is immeasurable and immovable. Every night I prayed for this. Be careful what you ask for!

what we hope for and certain of what we do not see."

With immigration and home-study papers in hand, I headed out to meet my children. After thirty hours, our team landed late at night at the Freetown airport, so meeting the children would have to wait until morning. Sleeping that night was almost impossible. While I've locked away so many of the feelings of these next three years deep in my heart, that first meeting lives vividly in my memory. I can see parts of it as clearly as I see myself in the mirror. God gave me the gift of that day to sustain me, to come back to, to cling to when all seemed dark and lost.

I had a few anxious moments before I met them. Would they like me? Would we connect? I especially worried about meeting Melvin. He was the oldest and the leader of his brothers and sister. If he didn't approve of me, what then?

The one hundred or so children at The Raining Season had all lined up in the driveway dressed in white T-shirts, red bandanas, and cowboy hats, all ready for us American ladies to meet them. As soon as they saw us, they began singing, "We welcome you in the name of Jesus Christ. You are precious in the sight of God . . ." I spotted Salieu first, who was out front with the little ones. We just grabbed each other and hugged and laughed and held on as we walked up the driveway. Kadiatu came out next grinning from ear to ear. I had written a letter to the children, so they knew that the Jones family from America was sponsoring them and that I was coming to see them. I had photos of all eight pinned to my shirt. Once we reached the gate of the compound, the children sang a new song, "This is our house, our home, we welcome you, yes, we welcome you . . ."

I could see Melvin in the distance. Kids were all around as we were ushered inside and upstairs so it wasn't until we were in a gathering room that our eyes met. He studied me. I will never forget the look in his eleven-year-old eyes. He saw into my soul. All at once, a decade of love and memories lost with this child were poured into me. I could feel it physically. I can't describe it any other way but to say love came down like a rushing waterfall upon my heart and soul. Worries melted as I stared into his eyes. Relief. Peace. Deep down I knew it would be that way. Mike and I had a lot to show them. We had to demonstrate what love really is. We had to gain trust. It would be a long time before we officially told them we were going to adopt them, but Melvin knew it in his heart right then . . . in fact, most of them did. From day one, we were always called Mom and Dad. God had given them peace, comfort, and belonging even before we could announce it to them.

Meeting, touching, hugging my children gave me the strength to fight, as somehow I knew it would be a battle. Leaving ten days later was heartbreaking, but I left knowing I would soon be back. I left knowing how hard I would fight to bring my children home and that this good-bye was temporary. But for them, I am sure they had many questions. When would I return? Would I really call? Would I really write? Is this love really real? It would become the first of many times I had to leave them behind. I did come home with a complete and total peace about bringing my family home. Yes, these were now my children. God ordained that moment to give me the fuel it would take to fight such a battle.

> It would be a long time before we officially told them we were going to adopt them, but Melvin knew it in his heart right then . . . in fact, most of them did. From day one, we were always called Mom and Dad.

My heart was full after that first trip. After I'd looked into their eyes and hugged my children, a resolve grew. Our good friend and Sunday school teacher had asked us to share our whole story with the class. Our whole story. The hard stuff, our marriage's redemption, the journey now. So much for keeping things inside. But we knew we'd need the support of friends throughout this journey. "Okay, God, You're going to have to give us the words." There was just too much to write out, including all the feelings I'd have to talk about, so we just shared. Feelings! Sharing! Oh, help. We sat (thank goodness) in chairs in the middle of a class of about twenty-five couples. Mike spoke first, starting with his wild times at UT. For one very intense hour, Mike told about our separation, his family's financial loss, and his prayer. I shared about my recent trip and the deep connection I had with our kids the minute I met them.

Of course, we cried. Our friends cried. It was a relief to have our whole story out there. We also told them the next steps, but that we didn't know how long it would take. We never thought it would take three years or that our journey would throw me into darker, heart-wrenching places than I could have imagined. Looking back, if I had put all my weight on feelings, I couldn't have survived what was to come.

At the time, there was a hold on adoptions in Sierra Leone while the government investigated adoptions from one agency almost a decade prior. The government's biggest fear was trafficking. We were told by someone in the government that this hold would be lifted very soon. Maybe next month. Surely by the end of that year. This was 2010.

After that first trip, I also told my teacher friends during a thirty-minute lunch period in one of our kindergarten classrooms about the adoption. These six women I'd taught with for about six years had known my struggle to leave my boys and go to work. Were they ever surprised to see me leave them for a ten-day trip across the world!

"You guys know I went on a trip. It was a mission trip,

but there's another reason that I went," I said. "We're adopting. I went to see my kids." As with my parents, I showed photos I'd taken so I could gradually say the number of children. My sweet friends squealed, laughed, and asked me about the kids and my trip.

"You'd be so proud of me, I didn't even take wipes," I said, poking fun at myself since they knew what a fanatic I was about keeping things clean. Actually, I never once thought about germs while I was in Sierra Leone. You just can't do that there. God ended that in me. Okay, so I don't let my kids lick off the floor and I still like to keep things clean, but no more wipes at restaurants. Each trip would change me more. The importance of it overrode any concerns I had about dirt.

I teared up telling them about Mike's prayer. They, similar to everyone I told who knew him, never would have pictured him like that, so broken. They knew we didn't know how it was going to work. They'd been to our house. They knew we didn't have tons of money. It would be faith. But they were right there with me.

In the meantime, we studied all about the adoption law in Sierra Leone and what changes the government was thinking of making to it. We learned that time spent in-country with the children would be imperative because they would need to see our commitment. There were rumors that the country would ratify the Hague Convention and come out with a new law. We began our search for a Sierra Leoneon attorney. We met with Sierra Leone government officials to ask whom they would recommend for our case. The Raining Season worked tirelessly to gather background information on our children to present to the courts. They got all the paperwork needed and then some.

Mike and I and the boys would Skype every weekend with the children, and I e-mailed a letter to them every single week for the entire duration of the adoption process. I later learned very few of these letters made their way to them, as Internet service was spotty and staff couldn't always relay messages. Skype was a blessing and a curse. I couldn't sleep well the night before a planned Skype session, wondering whether the children would have Internet connection, and my excitement thinking about seeing and talking to them kept me awake. My heart would soar when everything worked and I could see them, but afterward those feelings would come crashing down. It made me miss them even more. Each week I would take photos of the things Mike, Tyler, Tucker, and I would do. I would put these photos in an e-mail to send to them. I wanted the children to know us, what we did, what life was like here, and our everyday activities. I sent pictures of Tyler's school and Mike's office. I wanted them to know everything they could about us.

We knew we needed support and to raise money to remodel our house and create more bedrooms. So we shared in various adult Sunday school classes. The reactions to our story were mixed. I will never forget one man's response after we had spoken in his class. He came to us outside the classroom, perhaps with a look of pity. We had been crying; our conviction was still so fresh.

"We just know," we told him. "We just have to trust. We just have to have faith."

He said, "That sounds great, but the reality is you don't have the money."

I'm not sure what all he said after that because his words struck me and I was overcome with such sadness for him. I believe he represents the thoughts of many people. My heart immediately hurt for him because, although he was fellow Christian, he completely missed what we were trying to communicate. He really didn't think we should do it. He had just heard us say that God told us to do this. We were obeying God. I think I just stared at him. He didn't think God was big enough or powerful enough, or maybe he didn't think God actually worked in the everyday details of things, those big and small.

Whatever it was, all of those things are wrong. Reality is what God says, not man. Matthew 6 contains verses we cling to everyday. Jesus said, "Look at the birds of the air; they do not sow or reap or store away in barns, and yet your heavenly Father feeds them. Are you not much more valuable than they? Can any one of you by worrying add a single hour to your life?" (vv. 26–27). We can't worry. We just have to trust God; He's got this. That is what faith is.

The year ended with no new law and no movement on our adoption. We learned to take what was said in Sierra Leone with a grain of salt. I have often compared it to the old show *The Twilight Zone* because time is not important there. A date means absolutely nothing. Here, you say you'll do something on a certain day and you do it. There, you set up a meeting and they may never show up. That's normal, not rude. We learned if they said, "We will have this for you tomorrow," it meant absolutely nothing. It could be a year from then. Not one thing would happen like we thought it should happen.

11

Work, Pray, Work

(Mike)

There is a time for everything,
and a season for every
activity under heaven.

—

Ecclesiastes 3:1

In January 2011, Hayley made her second trip. Two months later she stayed home and I flew over to finally meet the children. I couldn't get enough of them. They hung on me so tightly while I was there. They were my shadow. And Kadiatu was my princess. It was so special having a daughter . . . a sweetness I had never known. The little ones loved my shaved head and touched it constantly. Our oldest children, Melvin, Yusufu, Kadiatu, and Peter, made the huge, life-changing decision to be baptized in the ocean, and I had the honor and privilege of being a part of it. They were petrified to go under the water, the same waters that had taken their biological father. Their thoughts raced as they walked out in that ocean, but their faith was stronger than their fears.

Hayley, at home, e-mailed me on March 4, 2011.

Mike,
I was wide awake this morning at 5:40 our time and the first thought was to pray HARD for you and the kids. So I did! I trust God that these prayers are HEARD and ANSWERED.

Can't wait to see your face but I know how TORN you will feel. It is nice that now we have both experienced that. I can't wait to see your pictures and video of the trip.

Tell them Mommy sends ALL her LOVE to THEM!
—HJ

While there, I hired our first attorney, someone who had been recommended to us. He promised to get us what we needed to get to court, but those promises would turn out to be empty words. I also met with more government officials, trying to figure out what we needed to do. We wanted to create a good relationship and have everything ready for when the time came to process the adoption. Still, nothing changed. The hold on adoptions was not getting lifted. They told us again, "Be patient. It will be very soon."

At home, Hayley wrote this e-mail to her sister living in South Africa one night after I gave her the bad news.

Courtney,
Well, here I sit in my pitch black room totally broken. Not sure what words to say. The only thing I keep thinking is ***broken***. It's funny how last night I laid in this same pitch black room and had the best conversation with Jesus. And tonight, I feel as though the weight of the unknown may crush me. For the

very first time I am unable to suppress all the emotions I feel. The fact that I have children, my children, stuck in an orphanage around the world. Right now, they are without water and they are without soap. They watched their first movie yesterday and the oldest four, well, Mike got to help baptize them today. They are not strangers in pictures or names on paper; they are my children. I sang praises with them and prayed with them and tucked them in bed. I read books to them, many, many books. I looked over all their schoolwork and we discussed their lessons. I have scratched their backs, taught them songs, played games with them, and held their hands. I have kissed their boo boos, wiped their runny noses, and tasted their sweat and tears on my lips.

And now, here I am, with nothing to hold but the memories. I must wake up tomorrow with my game face on. Go and face the day ahead like I am whole. I am not whole but Jesus is filling me.

I miss you and wish you were here. It felt good to type this . . .

I love you more than words,

—Hayley Beth

Courtney responded with just the right words:

Because of the LORD's great love we are not consumed,
for his compassions never fail.
They are new every morning;
great is your faithfulness.
I say to myself, "The LORD is my portion;
therefore I will wait for him."
(Lamentations 3:22–24)

As I prayed for you over "my" day, this was the verse that kept coming to mind. I was thinking of you going to bed broken and felt you needed this reminder . . . His mercies are NEW every morning!
Love,
Courtney

I said good-bye to the children and got to the airport, only to find out my flight was delayed a day. I mentally prepared myself to leave, so honestly, I felt like I'd been kicked in the teeth. I dreaded having to go back to the center and face a second good-bye. But it was a godsend that I got one more day to love on my kids and one more night to have prayer and worship with them and put them to bed. At least now I understood Hayley's empty feeling coming home. We could share it together and hopefully make the load a little lighter for each other.

On the way home I was hopeful that the lawyer we hired was going to work on getting us to court and that the kids would be home before we knew it. Throughout this whole process, we always had the feeling we were almost done and the end would be near, over and over, and over again. Within the next month, we had sent a letter of intent to the Ministry of Social Welfare through our attorney there and were being "patient." It was a difficult time because everyone at home wondered why we weren't we getting anywhere.

We traveled down this road with a handful of other families trying to adopt in Sierra Leone. All of us had been called by God and were allowing Him to lead us. These families would be our lifeline. When no one else understood us, they did. Journeying through these dark days with others has bound us together forever. Cords were twined so tightly they cannot be undone. Through joy and pain, they understood. We will forever love these people.

Throughout this whole process, we always had the feeling we were almost done and the end would be near, over and over, and over again.

Our church held a fundraiser for us in April. By now, we had flown to Sierra Leone three times, and Hayley was planning to go again that summer. Flights were anywhere from $1,800 to $2,900. We were still waiting for the government there to do something. Anything. We started remodeling the house soon after committing to adopt our kids, so from the very beginning we knew God was telling us to adopt them, and we felt a little like Noah building the ark with no rain in sight. We didn't know when God's promise would come true; we just had to get to work.

After that school year was over, Hayley resigned from her teaching job. It made finances tight, but we thought God was going to break this thing wide open one way or another, and she couldn't start a school year and then have to stop. That wouldn't be fair to the kids in her class. And if the children came home soon, she would need to be home with them. Or if the adoption stalled any longer, we thought she might have to go and live there to have time in-country to get them home on a relative visa. Hayley headed back to Sierra Leone in June 2011 and planned to stay a few weeks. She stayed until August.

The summer 2011 trip was different and gave us some real hope. Our three oldest children might have a chance to come home as part of a performing group that would travel the United States for six months raising awareness for the organization. A studio was offering to put together performances, a private school had stepped up to offer free education for them while they were in the States, and a record label had put together a venue and created some materials.

This was exciting, but it was complicated. Very complicated. Three children could come, but we had five more. What if the government still wasn't processing adoptions after the six-month visit? Imagine what taking them back would do.

The plan was that someone from the government in Sierra Leone would fly over with the children in the performing group, and while she was in the United States, she would meet with adoptive families and take back a report. This would be instrumental in getting adoptions opened up again, or so we were told. All was approved on the Sierra Leoneon side and now we just waited for the U.S. Embassy visa appointment for these children. Progress was made. Praise the Lord for this step!

One of the complications was the issue of health insurance while they were here living with us for those six months. Would the children be covered? We spent much time and money talking with different international attorneys, but they all said different things and did not know much about Sierra Leone. And we worried about the other five children. This needed serious prayer. Did we deny three children an opportunity because there were five more? Our hearts were torn, confused. Meanwhile, The Raining Season started a big media campaign to educate people in Sierra Leone about adoption. Ads in newspapers, interviews on TV and radio, and adopted children wrote into the newspaper to tell about their lives.

Melvin had a dream while Hayley was there that summer that made me cry. In his dream, he was standing in front of a big river. He could not get across, but he wanted to very badly. All of a sudden, a giant tree fell and made a bridge across the water. He and the kids were a little scared to walk on the tree, but they did and made it across. He said he knew he would make it across the water to America.

Hayley e-mailed me July 7, confused about what to do with the performance group and what this type of visa would mean in the long run.

> Mike,
>
> I am at my breaking point this morning. I am so devastated and confused and want to bawl my eyes out, but people are here and I don't want to do that. I want you here with me so bad. You REALLY NEED to talk to an international attorney from our area. Student visa can be used if we find an accredited school that they can go to. The thing there is, will they be on insurance? Can we count as dependents . . . I would think so. I am petrified that our kids will have to stay here. Reading with Melvin yesterday the smell of marijuana was taking my breath away. A group of men were sitting outside smoking joints. [The staff] talked to them and they said they had nothing else to do. There are no jobs, no money,

no food. What are they supposed to do? I know you have work today, but I can't get in touch with an international attorney. Talk to the church, maybe someone there can help us. Meeting with minister today. PRAY THAT he lets us adopt. Saw this verse laying on the table yesterday:

> I am the good shepherd. The good shepherd lays down his life for the sheep . . . I lay down My life for the sheep. But I have other sheep that are not of this fold; I must bring them also, and they will listen to My voice. Then there will be one flock, one shepherd. (John 10:11, 15b–16 HCSB)

Wow, what a verse. I LOVE YOU! I will let you know how the minister meeting goes. Please pray for me; I am really struggling here.

—HJ

12

When Months Turn into Years

(Hayley)

In the same way, the Spirit helps us
in our weakness. We do not know
what we ought to pray for,
but the Spirit himself intercedes for us
with groans that words cannot express.

—

Romans 8:26

I had missed the entire summer with Tyler and Tucker. Me, the mom who had cried leaving my baby in day care next to my classroom while I taught, was now away from my babies for months at a time. It's amazing how God really does give the strength to get through each day . . . and no more than that. Tyler, then six, was having a hard time. I was having a hard time. Tucker was still so little I feared he would forget me. Mike needed a wife. But being home only took the pain away from Tyler and Tucker. It left the other eight children hurting. And no matter where I was, I was torn. Completely torn. I continued to hide my emotions even more, to lock my feelings deep down inside.

Skyping with Mike and the boys was a blessing and a curse. Tyler would talk with me a little, but Tuck would sometimes stay outside the room, just close enough to hear my voice. Afterward, it would ruin the day if I thought too much about home and all that was happening there. So I had to cut something loose in my brain or I would lose it. I had to put a cap on the homesick, missing-my-family emotion or I couldn't function. All those times I was gone, my parents and Yay Yay and Grandpa gave Tyler and Tucker a happy place to stay during Mike's workdays. They kept the prayers going and the atmosphere light.

When I came home, it became harder to be here in America, surrounded by first-world problems. I wouldn't want to be here with everything America has and then hear people talk about problems. *Oh, just shut up!* I would yell in my mind. *You have no idea!*

Life is so hard in Sierra Leone, but simple and pure. I loved the market with thousands of people filling the streets of Freetown. Often being the only white lady there, I was a curiosity. I'm a huggy, touchy person, so I had fun meeting people, whether they knew English or not. People in the government speak English, but people in Freetown speak Krio. I learned a lot about the churches there as I'd go with different staff members from TRS, where I stayed in the guest house. I loved scrubbing laundry on a washboard in a big plastic tub and making meals, which is ten times harder to do there than here. Mostly, I learned that I was a whole lot happier with a whole lot less.

As time passed and I stayed prayerfully hopeful and faithful to the call, I kept thinking that I had learned a great lesson—that of patience, trust, and endurance. What more could there be? Why did I have to keep traveling around this same mountain going nowhere? I got it already. I got what I was supposed to do and I saw God is in control. So why was I still stuck in the same place? I still don't really know the answer. We will never fully understand God's ways; if we could, He wouldn't be that great of a God, would He?

I started to retreat into my shell. I just wanted to hide from the world, hide my pain. I felt certain no one would understand it. As much as my mom would have loved for me to reach out to her for comfort, I didn't. My nature, as I've said, is to keep most things to myself. And, honestly, there was no comfort. I told her once, "Mom, you don't understand. When I'm here, I can't stand it because my children are there. When I'm there, I can't stand it because my children are here."

I did have a remarkable time with the children that summer. If I wasn't in an adoption meeting, I was helping them at school. I mothered Mohammed after he broke his arm playing, and it took three days to get medical help and a cast. One day I decided to take them to their first restaurant in Freetown. It was called Montana Garden, and the menu actually had a picture of a scene from Montana. So strange, the things you see there. The children were at the guest house with me and were excited to go out. I asked Melvin to wash his hands and face and then I heard the shower running. (It was one of those times when we actually had running water.) He felt his first drop of warm water and loved it. We "dressed up." The boys had jeans I had brought them and shirts with no holes. I painted Kadiatu's nails.

At the restaurant, they did not know what anything was or how to order, and I could tell Melvin was worried about not knowing things. He said he wanted pizza. There were about thirty kinds, and they all sounded weird to me, but I could not describe them to him because they call those foods different names, so saying "mushrooms," for example, meant nothing to him. We decided on pepperoni pizza.

They brought out the food, and the children just sat and looked. Melvin really watched me with a worried, uncomfortable look. I put a piece on his plate, and he still waited. It was pizza, which most kids just pick up and shove in their mouths, but they wanted to use the silverware. I started cutting mine, and I saw Melvin awkwardly pick up his knife and fork. And it hit me. My twelve-year-old son had never used a fork or a knife. In their village, they used their hands. At TRS, only spoons were available. I tried to cut slowly so he could figure it out by watching me, but it was all new, holding the fork and trying to cut with the knife. So I took his hands and showed him. I hurt for him so badly. Then I got each of

> After three months there, let me tell you there are no words to capture the pain of having to walk away from your children and leave them in an orphanage in a third-world country.

them strawberry and vanilla swirl ice cream. "It is so cold and sweet," they said. We walked on the beach afterward, and they were so excited when I bought each of them necklaces for a dollar a piece. Back at the guest house for bedtime prayers, I thanked God for that wonderful night. I felt totally blessed.

I thought I knew how hard good-byes could be. But after three months there, let me tell you there are no words to capture the pain of having to walk away from your children and leave them in an orphanage in a third-world country. With each visit, trust was gained, love was grown, hearts were softened, and souls were healed . . . little by little. Each time we had to part was gut wrenching, especially after long stays like this one. People handle pain in different ways, and that includes the children. Some would withdraw the day of good-bye and try to push away the pain. Others would follow my every step, lie in my arms, and cry uncontrollably. I spent much time sitting in silence, holding my children as their tears poured down like rain. And others would cling to me until the last minute when their hands were pried from my shirt. Good-byes were hard for everyone, even the staff who were left with heartbroken children. Each time when the big gate of the compound would slam shut, so would a part of my soul.

I had to return to the United States a couple of weeks before the visa appointment that would give the three oldest permission to travel to the United States as part of the performance group. Looking back on this now, I knew something was wrong. Very wrong. But hindsight is 20/20. Leaving after three months was the worst yet, but now the three oldest had hope. We made a calendar counting down the days until they came home. Our house was a remodeling disaster. We would just have to make do all cozied up together when they came home until the rooms were ready.

The performance group interviewed for their visas at the U.S. Embassy August 10, 2011. What happened in that room is a mystery. Their file was not even opened. The children were denied the visas to come perform. "God, why?" We were heartbroken and angry, but not surprised. All that work, all those documents put together, and they were not even opened. This group had been our best hope to get all of our children home. We had expected a government official to visit America to see the group perform, which should have led to opening up adoptions. Now what? My three oldest, counting down the days, had been so close.

I Skyped with Melvin, Yusufu, and Kadiatu after the visa denial. It was a moment in my life I never want to go back to again. Their pain and mine was unreal. We spoke very little, and just stared at each other, unable to draw a breath without hurting. It was sadness, a defeat beyond words. We physically hurt, all three children and me. We couldn't be together. We couldn't sit in the same room or hold each other in silence for comfort, so we did the best we could; we stared into each other's eyes and longed for so much more. This was a breaking point for me and brought about my downward spiral into dark depths that I hope I never return to.

Fighting for the orphan is at the center of God's heart and a battle that is constantly raging. I had to believe that He used that situation and would use all of our efforts to complete His perfect will, although it was not the way we had hoped. We were well aware our ways are not His. Our only rest was knowing that we had left no stone unturned.

After this, it became hard for me to even breathe. My every thought was consumed by my children, who would go to bed another night alone, without a hug or kiss or hearing, "I love you." They would wake up each day and have to face it alone. I had a hard time being around people. I wanted to avoid the world. What would they ask me? What would I say? I would be in the store and look around at all the "stuff" and want to break down. *Who needs all this stuff?* In Sierra Leone, I lived without electricity, running water, and only had the bare necessities and made it just fine. Now I was in America listening to people complain about the silliest things. Parents worried about what matching outfit and hair bow to get; my children were stuck in a third-world country fighting over who would get to wear one of the few pairs of underwear. Parents filled bubble baths for their kids; I prayed mine were able to fetch water somewhere so they could get a sponge bath out of a bucket. Parents purchased yummy meals for their kids; I trusted God that mine would get fed. Parents set rules to help keep their children safe; I pleaded with God to keep the enemy away from mine.

My world was in pieces, shambles, but I knew I shouldn't hold it against unknowing people here. That's not what God would want. But I struggled. I felt so very lonely, even with Mike by my side. Nighttime was the worst. With Tyler and Tucker in bed, my mind would spin. I poured my heart out to God every single night. I prayed for my children's hearts, minds, and bodies, that He would put a wall of protection around each of them. As much as we trusted and believed in The Raining Season, life in an orphanage in a third-world country is still full of dangers. I cried every night. Mike wisely knew there was absolutely nothing he could say to make it any better, so he let me grieve. There were times that reminded him of our separation. He was lonely, even when I was right next to him. The evilness of situation after situation we faced in Sierra Leone was taking me away from us here, and Mike still had to get

My world was in pieces, shambles, but I knew I shouldn't hold it against unknowing people here. That's not what God would want. But I struggled. I felt so very lonely.

up and go to work as though everything was fine.

I couldn't get through the day without reading these three passages from the book of Psalms.

Turn to me and be gracious to me,
for I am lonely and afflicted.
The troubles of my heart have multiplied;
free me from my anguish.
Look upon my affliction and my distress
and take away all my sins.
See how my enemies have increased
and how fiercely they hate me!
Guard my life and rescue me;
let me not be put to shame,
for I take refuge in you. (25:16–20)

I am still confident of this:
I will see the goodness of the LORD
in the land of the living.
Wait for the LORD;
be strong and take heart
and wait for the LORD. (27:13–14)

The righteous cry out, and the LORD hears them;
he delivers them from all their troubles.
The LORD is close to the brokenhearted

> and saves those who are crushed in spirit. (34:17–18)

I came across some notes I had put in my Bible from a sermon I had heard. They resonated with me.

> If you are *determined*, God will give you favor wherever you go. *All* things are possible with God. No matter what we come up against, never say there is no way. Jesus said, "I am the way." God likes *determined* people. When the devil says it will be this way, say flee from me in seven ways. You will have a billion opportunities to give up; that's the enemy trying to *destroy your destiny*. Luke 5:18–20 talks about the paralytic man and how his friends did not give up; in fact, they tore off the roof! Jesus was so impressed by their *determination* and the lengths they would go to that He gave them what they wanted. Sometimes when we have a disadvantage, we give up. Zacchaeus was too short to see Jesus, but he was *determined* and looked for a way. He had to climb the tree, but it worked and he got what he wanted. Mark 10:46 begins the story of the blind beggar. He was at a disadvantage but cried out even louder, doing all he could and Jesus heard him and said, "Your faith has healed you" (v. 52). Beethoven's teacher

told him he was hopeless as a composer and Henry Ford failed and went into bankruptcy five times before he succeeded. These people had *determination* and were willing to do whatever it took. God likes *determined* people.

We were determined.

I found comfort in the story of Elijah praying for rain in 1 Kings 18. Elijah, embracing God's promise of rain, "bent down to the ground and put his face between his knees" (v. 42). He sent his servant to look toward the sea seven times. "The seventh time the servant reported, 'A cloud as small as a man's hand is rising from the sea'" (v. 44). The sky grew black, the wind rose, and a heavy rain came . . . just as God had promised Elijah. So we continued to pray and looked to the horizon, again and again. We waited, certain of the promise of God.

13

The Breaking Point

(Hayley)

I love the Lord, for he heard my voice;
he heard my cry for mercy.

—

Psalm 116:1

By fall 2011, we were tired of the government breaking its promises to process our adoption. If one more person told me to be patient, I would have screamed. "Next month," they would say, "next month." We'd been patient for more than a year, and nothing had changed. No new law, no movement. And now the minister of social welfare, who would not allow adoptions to be processed, had been fired. No one was immediately named to replace him, so we were in a holding pattern.

The kids were really struggling and couldn't understand why this was happening. They desperately wanted to come home. We Skyped with them every Saturday and sent an e-mail every week. And Kadiatu sent us an e-mail that broke us. She wrote, "I will gather up all my courage because I have faith in the God I serve that he will answer my prayers and I will cross the sea just like Moses did." And yes, those were all her words! That pretty much sums up these kids. We are so blessed by them.

We were like hamsters in a wheel, spinning ourselves incessantly and going nowhere. And I knew nobody at an official level cared. I could not count how many times I had heard that I could have a certain paper by such-and-such day, and then, you've guessed it, the paper wasn't ready. That's why I had to go to Sierra Leone so many times, to stay visible, to build relationships that are so important to life there.

Despite all the frustrations, my love for Sierra Leone, called *Salone* by its people, continued to grow. I felt like I belonged there. Cherry, a cab driver the center often hires, was usually behind the wheel taking me to government offices or to meet a lawyer. He became a friend and a lifesaver. Staff at the center, which was now my second home, became my family. They even approved my attempt at making cassava, which to me looked like spinach but had a different taste.

> It just as easily could have been me born poor in a third-world country. We are no better; we have just lived in different circumstances, and only God knows why.

At times I was lonely, but I learned a lot about myself, especially what I need in life and what I don't. I was much stronger than I'd ever imagined. I truly enjoyed going to the big outdoor market and haggling prices with vendors. I wanted people I met to know their value as I looked them in the eyes, touched them. I believed it just as easily could have been me born poor in a third-world country and they could be in my shoes. We are no better; we have just lived in different circumstances, and only God knows why. I felt a comfort fetching water, making meals, taking our bucket baths at night. On those occasions when water was running at the center, it was freezing. So we would boil water for one bucket and add cooler water and had another bucketful to rinse out shampoo. If the generator at the building behind us was working, the neighbor's light made it feel like bathing by moonlight.

I unintentionally lost weight every time I was there, which worried my mom. Mike would say I looked like a skeleton. Food there isn't for enjoyment like it is here. I ate what I could, which generally wasn't very much. I would bring snack bars for extra nutrition, but once I ran out, there was no convenience store on the corner to get more. On one trip I caught an eye disease and came home with an angry red blob on my eye. Lack of food and stress made my hair fall out by the handfuls and my nails break off. None of that mattered to me. I knew on every trip that I was exactly where I was supposed to be. That was God's gracious peace.

Though I saw dreaded darkness and evil, I also saw opportunity for God to show up miraculously. I had read about demon possession in the Bible, and I had heard about witchcraft, but now I witnessed exorcisms and saw the fear curses brought among people. I saw things that I couldn't call home and talk about. Only those there with me could understand. But the darker the night, the brighter the light shines. I couldn't get through those days without being armed with my psalms. They're embedded in me: I will wait for the Lord. I will be strong, take heart, and wait for the Lord. The Lord will hear me. He will deliver me from all my troubles. The Lord is close to the brokenhearted and will save those who are crushed in spirit.

Every trip, my relationship with my children grew deeper. During the day, I did whatever I could to work on their adoption, and at night the children and I went over schoolwork, played, and hung out. Getting to know them and their friends made this time priceless. Building this relationship with them was the blessing found in the long road to bringing them home. All this time in-country with them would pay off.

I clung to one of many sweet memories. Every night, about one hundred orphaned children would gather for evening prayer. This was my favorite time with the kids. They would sing and worship, hear a short Bible lesson, and then pray. Their prayers made my heart sing. I could only imagine the smile they brought to God's face. After a particularly long, hot day, all were gathered in one big room. My littles were snuggled up next to me. We were sweaty, dirty, and smelly, but it didn't matter, not at all. They ran their little fingers through my hair, rubbed my arms, and picked at what was left of my pink toenail polish. They studied me, and I studied them. They had found comfort in me, a trust. Though I had to leave them many times, I had always returned for them and was continuing to fight for them.

One evening I felt eyes staring at me, and I looked up. Melvin sat over to the side. This same boy who saw into my soul the first moment I met him was searching me again. He watched and smiled as his little brothers loved on me. I knew his mind was deep in thought. He was quiet as I put him in bed, and he hugged me extra tightly that night. The next morning he left me a note, all folded up and addressed, "To My Mommy." It contained the most beautiful words: ". . . thank you for what you are doing for us. You make our world beautiful." That is what I was fighting for. I had heard the phrase "you can't change the whole world, but you can change one person's whole world," and believed in that truth. As I studied Melvin's letter I thought, *Oh dear child, you have no idea what you are doing to my world. Praise God mine will never be the same.* I have seen the love of God. Even through the pain and struggle, these children had already made my world more beautiful than I ever imagined it could be.

That fall back in the United States after yet one more delay, I hit a huge breaking point. My heart had had enough. I was no longer able to do this. During that dark year, it was hard to pray full thoughts. The emptiness was so raw, I couldn't put it into words. Mike tried but couldn't comfort me. My parents couldn't comfort me. My boys would hug me, and I would buck up for them and try to say a positive prayer. I didn't want them to see me so down.

One day I knew I had to get Tucker down for a nap before I fell apart. As he slept with a baby's peace in his room, I fell on my knees in my bedroom and threw my hands in the air and cried aloud, "God, You know I cannot do this anymore!" And I'm not one to say I can't do something. I felt His presence standing right behind me. I knew He was right there with me, watching me. Words flooded into my soul: *I will answer your prayer*. I immediately stood up. That petrifying, sad feeling that had dominated me was completely gone. It was over. That dark year of sadness was over, and the despair immediately lifted.

Hebrews 11:1 is my favorite verse: "Now faith is being sure of what we hope for and certain of what we do not see." Those comforting words from God became my battle cry.

God didn't say my prayer would be answered right away, but He said He would answer it. That was all I needed. It would actually be another year and a half before the children would come home, but the struggle was different. I could always go back to that moment when God showed me His love and promise. He reminded me not to lose hope! And I never went back to that sad, zombie stage.

Another trip in November ended at another wall. How many times could I sit in the same government offices waiting on them to keep their word? How many different people did I have to talk to? We looked for different lawyers in Sierra Leone. One attorney told me to "just pick two kids, any two" and then asked to be paid just to tell us how much he would charge us for our case. Um, no thanks. Another lawyer was sitting at his desk in a suit coat and tie but was not wearing any pants below his desk! Never a dull moment. We strengthened our case by completing DNA tests to prove the identities of the children's living relatives and then met with all of those relatives again to be sure everyone agreed with our adoption.

Faith sustained us and got me through the day. We celebrated another Christmas without them. As I mentioned earlier, Hebrews 11:1 is my favorite verse: "Now faith is being sure of what we hope for and certain of what we do not see." Those comforting words from God became my battle cry. I told Mike several times that I wanted *Faith* tattooed on me to have a permanent, visual reminder. I wanted to look at it and claim it. On my thirtieth birthday in March 2012, Mike said, "Let's go get that tattoo." *Faith* is now forever inside my left wrist, in black ink, for me to see every time I look down. That same day Mike had *Eph 5:25* tattooed on his ring finger, like a wedding band, to remind him that a husband must love his wife the same way that Christ loved the church and gave His life for her.

When my mother first saw my tattoo (at church one Sunday morning), she asked me, "Are you sure you're always going to want that?"

My response was, "Faith? Yes, I am sure I will always want that." We had to laugh. The following week my dad let his sleeve scoot up to reveal *Faith* written across his wrist in Sharpie ink.

I went to Salone in April 2012, then again that summer. I was so full of determination that I knew I would stay as long as it took to get the adoption through court. We needed another lawyer, and God sent us one. Once again, I had to explain about wanting to adopt eight children. He sat and listened. I had met so many corrupt lawyers, but this man was different. I had peace that could only come from God. I trusted. Terrified, I felt like my life was in his hands. Trusting anyone in that country was incredibly difficult after everything that had happened. But he believed in what we were doing and wanted our family to be together. I was in his office many times over the next few months.

Mike and I knew it would be difficult to convince a judge we could handle raising eight children, so we worked diligently on proving our home to be sound, our relationship to be strong, and ended up filing for adoption of the children in two groups, hoping that would make it easier for the judge to approve. We filed the adoption petition and then we waited. Months I waited in Salone. Away from Mike, Tyler, and Tucker, but with our other eight children. I mothered Peter through an eardrum rupture, Melvin through a sickness, and Salieu through a mild case of malaria.

As the months passed, people at home began to wonder. Family and a core group at church were firmly and faithfully with us, but others not so much. They questioned. They doubted. We heard the whispers. Most wouldn't say anything to our face. But some would. "This isn't God's will," they'd say. "It's not His plan because it is too difficult." Know this: Just because something is difficult does not mean it is not God's will. He refines us and tests us to teach us about ourselves. Life was not easy for most Bible heroes. Jesus dying on the cross was not easy, but it was always God's plan.

14

Home Front

(Mike)

Command those who are rich
in this present world not to be arrogant
nor to put their hope in wealth,
which is so uncertain, but to put their hope
in God, who richly provides us with
everything for our enjoyment.

—

1 Timothy 6:17

In the beginning, we had no idea our adoption would take three years. We believed each trip Hayley made (about eight all together) was going to mean progress, and we always had hope that it would happen next month, and then the next month. I made only one trip since I had about one week of vacation each year, and I wanted to save that time to spend with the kids when they got to come home, which, of course, we always hoped would be next month.

Hayley and I were both surviving our circumstances across the ocean. There would be one plan after another she'd try to execute that would only take things backward, or she would hurry up to wait on Sierra Leoneon time, which we've already related to living in *The Twilight Zone*. She looked like a corpse when we Skyped once a week, the adoption would be at a standstill, so I'd have to tell her it was time to come home for a while. It tore her up to have to leave. We prayed together when she came home from trips, but there was a burden on her that distanced us. She was here, but she wasn't.

There were two things we heard constantly during the

journey to bring the children home. People often say, "You must have a really big house." No, we do not. Our home started as a four-bedroom, one-story, ranch-style house built in the early 1980s. Sometimes people ask us outright how we were able to afford adopting eight and taking care of ten children. Others say to our parents or friends, "Oh, they must have a lot of money. What does he do for a living?" No, we are by no means wealthy—at all. I have a good job, and Hayley is a stay-at-home mom. The people who really know us knew these things, so I can only imagine some of their concerns.

> When people asked, "How will this work?" we just said, "I don't know." And, oh, the looks you get when you say you don't know.

We saved every penny. Literally, we rolled all of our change and took it to the bank. We were never big spenders, but now we didn't spend money on discretionary things. No Starbucks runs, no movies or dinners out. Hayley didn't get her hair done or get manicures or go shopping. Ever. I didn't hang out with buddies. Those things are not wrong. Please hear us: they are not wrong at all. We just made careful choices. God had changed our hearts and given us a new, different focus. We made a choice to accept this calling on our family. Whatever it took.

God told me He would provide as I buried my head in His feet during that life-changing prayer a few years earlier. He *did* provide. He said He would feed them. He *had* fed them. It wasn't my problem. When Hayley knew she should be a stay-at-home mom and cried out to Him, He told her, "It's not your problem; it's Mine."

When people asked, "How will this work?" we just said, "I don't know." And, oh, the looks you get when you say you don't know. Hayley remembers a statement she heard somewhere years before: God doesn't call the equipped; He equips the called. God didn't choose us because we were rich or prepared. We were the exact opposite. I'm not sure why God called us out for this. Maybe it was because we were crazy enough to dive right in and not look back. I do know God will never lead you somewhere and not give you all that you need along the way.

We needed to remodel our 2,400-square-foot house to make more room and figure out how to pay for the attorneys, all the trips to Sierra Leone, plane tickets to bring everyone home, as well as monthly sponsorships for all eight children until they were finally here. Our savings, family, and church support paid for Hayley's trips. For the final trip when everyone flew home, we raised some money on gofundme.com. Since this was an independent adoption, there were no big agency fees, so that worked in our favor. As time went on, though, the expenses grew. Thinking about the amount of money we would need to make life work for our family of twelve was almost mindboggling. But we knew living by faith wasn't about just one area of our life but our whole life, and finances are a part of that. It was very scary walking into the financial unknowns. We had no idea how it would be possible!

The downstairs, which had a door to the carport, had a closet-size laundry room, a recreational-vehicle size bathroom, a storage room, and the rest was unfinished concrete floors that kept my weight room equipment. We had to gut the 1,100 square feet downstairs to make more room and dig out about 183 wheelbarrows full of dirt. Upstairs, we removed the breakfast area to double the size of the kitchen. A family we didn't know happened to be remodeling their eight-year-old home in a suburb near us when they heard about us and donated their old cabinets (much bigger and nicer than what we had), their double ovens, a second dishwasher, and a microwave. Another family donated another washer and dryer. We didn't get a loan but used our savings, donations, and *lots* of donated labor. We saved tens of thousands of dollars with the help of a group of men called Carpenter's Hands at church, which upgraded the electrical panel at our house to meet our needs as well as the framing labor for remodeling the basement. My dad and my brother, Brian, donated countless hours. My brother would work on the house all day for weeks and months by himself on his time off from the fire hall while I was at work. We created more bedrooms, a TV/study room, and a full bath downstairs. The remodeling gave us close to 3,500 square feet of living space when we were done.

It is completely humbling to see how God raised up people to help us during this time. There were so many people who gave what they had to help our family. The missions department at church was able to pay the contractor to upgrade the septic at the house to accommodate the county requirements for our home modifications. The house looked like a construction zone for many months. During most of that time, Hayley was in Sierra Leone. Tyler, Tucker, and I scrounged around the living room trying to find plates, cups, and pantry items that were being stored while the kitchen was torn apart. Drywall dust covered everything we owned. It was a giant task, but we had a village of hard-working, dedicated people who kept us sane during this time. People collected clothing and donated furniture, many bunk beds, and eventually we had spots for everyone to lay their heads at night. The house was ready; it was just missing the souls to fill it.

After four months of Hayley being gone in summer 2012, I was worn out. I needed her home. And while we had much support, we also were receiving lots of opinions and questions. "Why is Hayley still there?" "When is she coming home?" "When are the children really coming?" I actually stopped going to church for a while, mostly to avoid people. I was tired of living as a family apart, tired of the emotional roller coaster, and tired of all the questions. I felt as though I was on the verge of snapping at the next person who brought it up. Some people didn't understand that for twenty-seven months or so we had been doing what God told our family to do. That was why we grew such strong relationships with those who were also trying to adopt. I didn't have to re-explain everything them. They understood the call.

When Hayley was home, she felt lonely. Isolated. She was here physically, but she was somewhere else. And she quickly got disgusted with American lifestyles. She wasn't hateful, but she was constantly aware of how others struggled for survival on the most minimal rations with no hope for tomorrow. Living in a third-world country makes our first-world problems seem petty. Many times her heart was in Sierra Leone while her empty frame was here. She loves Tyler and Tucker, but one child does not take the place of another. I couldn't do or say anything that brought her comfort, especially during 2011, what she calls her year of despair. She was like a stray ally cat with her fur standing straight up, not wanting to be petted. I feared I might get my eyes clawed out, so I gave her space.

When she was gone, my relationship with Tyler and Tucker grew, and I definitely felt closer to them. They clung to me because I was dad *and* mom for them. So I comforted them in a way that hadn't been my role and experienced a sweet tenderness I hadn't necessarily felt before. It was eye-opening to me how God made the roles of mom and dad to fill so many needs. And it was also heartbreaking to think about a single mother or father having to fill those different needs on a long-term basis. When Hayley came home, it was disturbing to think what our kids in Sierra Leone were going through and lacking when we left them there. The center was a good place compared to living on the streets, but staff couldn't fill the roles of a mother and father.

We both avoided answering e-mails sometimes. "No, we aren't all together yet." "Yes, delayed again." Since Middle Tennessee is home to so many adopted children, it was hard for people to understand why our adoption was so difficult. Most adoptive parents would work with an agency and have a referral for a child within a year, but we were still struggling to get Sierra Leone's adoption ban lifted. We heard that someone said, "It's just a pipe dream." And we heard other comments such as, "Why don't you just go to Ethiopia if you want to adopt?" Because God had told us to adopt *these* children. And He never told us anything different.

The summer 2012 trip had changed Hayley even more, opening her eyes to the unquenchable need. People think adopting eight children makes a huge impact, but we were only scratching the surface of the needs there. When you go on a mission trip, you see glimpses of poverty and pain, and it is eye-opening and can be life changing, but you are only experiencing part of the problem. When you spend an extended period of time in a place like Sierra Leone, you become more aware of the vastness of the needs and struggles and how complicated it can be trying to meet them. But Jesus lives there. He stares you in the face, asking for help through the eyes of His people. You just have to open your eyes to see Him!

When you spend an extended period of time in a place like Sierra Leone, you become more aware of the vastness of the needs and struggles and how complicated it can be trying to meet them.

Throughout the journey, we had Sunday school classes from several churches praying for us. People were curious about the crazy couple who wanted to adopt eight children, so we spoke to several groups. We told our story, how God chose us for these specific children and how He promised me that night in the bedroom floor that He would provide for us. They saw the tears of a man broken by God and two lives free-falling into complete trust in God. Many saw how God was going to use this story in mighty ways.

When Hayley was gone, sometimes for weeks or months, my parents and Hayley's parents helped care for the boys. Yay Yay and Grandpa told me the boys missed their mom, but they never had tears or tantrums when they were with them. The boys prayed with them for their whole family in Sierra Leone, "Jesus, help them get home."

15

Mighty Ways

(Hayley)

We live by faith, not by sight.

—

2 Corinthians 5:7

Mothering children on two different continents is not for the faint of heart. No matter where I was, some of my children were without me. When I was in Sierra Leone from June to September 2012, a couple of times a week I would hear that the court orders would be ready, but in the all-too-familiar pattern, the day would come and go with still nothing happening. Hoping the orders would come through, I would extend my trip and change plane tickets, as I had done countless times before. Everyone in that airline office in Freetown knew me by name. A sense of suffocation began to nag at me. After almost four months there, I could feel Satan trying to get in my head, in my heart, to fill me with doubts and fears that once again I would leave empty-handed.

Mothering children on two different continents is not for the faint of heart. No matter where I was, some of my children were without me.

As September came to an end, I had to go home, even

though the adoption court order was not yet in my hands. Tyler's eighth birthday was coming up. Almost every morning in Sierra Leone I would wake up knowing I was exactly where I was supposed to be, but one day I had a different feeling—I just knew I had to leave, even though it was going to crush me. Without God, I could not move. I had nothing left in me, and He was the only thing keeping me going, so I had to move with Him. Telling the children goodbye, again, broke me. It was a sadness that took my breath away. I returned home clinging to faith.

> God had overcome. He laughed at the talk of "Why don't you just choose other kids?" and "It's a pipedream" or "You know you can't afford this." Never tell God what is not possible.

All Tyler wanted that birthday was for me to come home. He needed me to tuck him in bed after a story, a song, and a prayer. He needed to come running in the house to tell me about what really cool insect he had found outside. He needed me to get him dressed for school in the morning, and he needed to see my face in the car-rider line to pick him up at the end of the day.

Being home with Mike and the boys was wonderful, but my mind and half of my heart was still in Salone. I felt so helpless being across the ocean, unable to talk to anyone, visit my attorney, or check up on the court order. Oh, we were so close! So very close to the finish line, and yet we were still helpless. Everything was out of our hands.

And then God moved.

I got an e-mail a few days after I came home. The court orders were signed, sealed, and delivered to the children's center! A Sierra Leoneon court had approved our adoption! TRS staff e-mailed the court documents to us, knowing it would take a little time to get the papers delivered to the States. I clicked open that e-mail and studied those adoption orders countless times. Each time I was as breathless as the first. Mike was at work, but we talked several times, and we could not believe that it was *finally* happening. It was surreal.

God had overcome. He laughed at the talk of "Why don't you just choose other kids?" and "It's a pipedream" or "You know you can't afford this." Never tell God what is not possible. It will make you look foolish. Jesus has the power to break every chain, every stronghold. "Greater is He who is in you than he who is in the world" (1 John 4:4 NASB). My incessant prayers for immeasurable and immovable faith were answered tenfold. I could laugh now and tell Mike, "I really think that prayer is why this took so long."

I felt calm while at the same time I was overjoyed—but without screaming or jumping up and down. If I'm completely honest, because of the emotional roller coaster we'd been on and having been burned so many times, I really thought some other bad news might come our way. It didn't feel safe to completely let my guard down. My children were not home yet. They were now legally ours, but we still worried and feared for their well-being and safety. My nights were still restless.

Because I knew God had done a great and mighty act, I should have been more jubilant, more exuberant, but I wouldn't let myself go that far. Maybe I was jaded from the past dealings with the country. Maybe I was afraid to release it all. Whatever it was, I was reserved. We called family members and told them the news, and they were thrilled. We thought within a month or two this would be over. Could they be home by Christmas?

We lived much of our lives just like we would when they came home. Every meal I would think about how much more I would make when they arrived. Every bedtime I thought about tucking them in. Every grocery store run I liked to imagine the chaos of them tagging along . . . or running uncontrollably through the store. Either thought brought a smile.

We had purchased a fifteen-passenger van, and every time I climbed up in that vehicle I glanced in the rearview mirror and pictured ten heads looking back at me. Planning for the children's homecoming kept my mind busy and gave me a sense of purpose. I would sit in their new bedrooms, lay my head on their beds, and arrange their clothes in the closets many times. It made me feel closer to them.

The pain was still there, trying to take hold of me, to rob me of my joy. I had two beautiful children here at home with me, and they deserved to have me present and engaged. I loved every minute with them. I soaked up the moments before the craziness of eight more kids came. Our little family of four made some special memories. The boys needed to know how much they were loved, how much they were valued and special. I wanted to focus fully on them these months before the other children arrived.

All we needed now were the kids' visas, which was permission from the U.S. Embassy that they could enter the United States. We were dealing with the United States now, so I thought I'd call the U.S. Embassy there and get the ball rolling. We thought they would just have to visit the village to talk with any living relatives, visit the children's center, basic due diligence. But as it turned out, I couldn't just call and talk to a counselor there. When I called, I got front office staff who were Sierra Leoneon. I'd explain what I needed, then I'd get transferred and have to explain again, and we went around in circles. I began to wonder if there were any Americans in the U.S. Embassy because I certainly couldn't get one on the phone. There was a general e-mail address, but no one responded to my messages. We contacted our senator, and family members reached out to anyone they knew with contacts in our government.

We were going to have to make this happen in person.

16

Coming Home

(Hayley)

Let us hold unswervingly
to the hope we profess,
for he who promised is faithful.

—

Hebrews 10:23

Since 2010, our Christmas cards had included photos of our Great Eight—no matter that they still lived 1,755 miles away. On 2012's card, after we'd finally been approved for adoption, Psalm 52:9 helped us say it: "I will praise you forever for what you have done" (HCSB).

After another frustrating phone call to the U.S. Embassy and no movement on the visas, I was sitting at the kitchen table again, praying. *Now what? Should we go ahead and buy the airplane tickets for all of us to come home? Should we wait? God, You've done so much.* And then I felt confident when I asked Him, *Show me something I can cling to, tell me what to do.* I opened my Bible: "Have you not heard? Long ago I ordained it. In days of old I planned it; now I have brought it to pass" (2 Kings 19:25). It was one of those exciting God moments, and I got right up to write it on the white board in the kitchen. The heaven-sent verse has been covered at Christmases with cards from friends and family, but those faded words are still there, reminding us that His plans happen! No, we didn't have visas, but God had planned it. He would bring it to pass. I called Mike, and we bought nine plane tickets right then for March 18, 2013, for our children to come home. And then we bought one more ticket for me for two weeks earlier to go get those visas.

God spoke His word to us through other people, reassuring us that this is His plan. During those six months of waiting on visas, a lady in my mom's Sunday school class knew our struggle and wrote a verse on a little piece of paper and gave it to my mom. The verse had helped her through rough times, and she felt like she should share it with me. "For the revelation awaits an appointed time; it speaks of the end and will not prove false. Though it linger, wait for it; it will certainly come and will not delay" (Habakkuk 2:3). Wait for it. It will come. I taped that little slip of paper to the dashboard in my van, and it stayed there until our eight came home.

By early March, I was in Sierra Leone going back and forth from The Raining Season to the U.S. Embassy. Since I was there in person, an American counselor was assigned to me. Once I talked to her, she was my angel. "This is wonderful," she said. "This is so great. Are your other kids excited?" She told me she would get to work on our visas and that I should come back in a few days. It seemed hard to believe. That's it? No more hoops to jump through? They had done their due diligence and sent out investigators to meet living relatives, check stories, and make sure everything was legitimate. Since international adoptions had been closed for years, the people there were figuring out their protocol. In turn, I tried to figure out what they had to do and put the pieces together. Wheels were finally turning.

We had become close with a couple from Kentucky who was adopting three children. They had arrived about a week earlier but were hitting a brick wall with visas. Both of our families were approved for adoptions and just needed the visas. But their counselor at the embassy had told them that no one was leaving; no one was getting visas. I had a different counselor and had just heard a completely different story. My elation turned to confusion. So I went back to the embassy to check. My counselor said it was still in the process, but it would take a few more days. I was used to delays, so this wasn't new.

I sent texts to Mike, letting him know I still didn't have visas as it got closer to March 18. We had planned for my dad to join me to help me travel home with the kids. The day before my dad was going to fly out, Mike let him know that he might not want to go because there were delays and we might not get the kids. My dad thought and prayed. He called Mike back. "I'm going," he said. "God hasn't told me it isn't going to happen."

Daddy had seen our Great Eight's photos many times and had Skyped with them once or twice. When he arrived at the orphanage, the kids ran to him, covering him with hugs and saying, "Grandfather, Grandfather." Knowing these kids so well and knowing my dad's nature, I expected that beautiful, sweet, precious moment. It just fit. My kids locked on to my dad, now called Poppy. They read to him and played soccer with him. "It was love right off the bat," he says. I wanted him to see and enjoy and take in each moment and notice the little things as I got to share my home away from home with him. One day we went into crowded downtown Freetown where women carry huge loads on their heads and *popo* (wrap) the babies around their waists. Kids were everywhere as most weren't in school. I loved seeing Daddy talking, smiling, and saying hello to anyone and everyone. Love is a language everyone understands.

> When God says it's time, then and only then is it time. And there is nothing you can do to stop it. Watching this miracle happen was almost like an out-of-body experience; it was all so unbelievable.

Our friends with me were still getting a constant no from their counselor at the embassy. Meanwhile, mine told me to come back on Thursday. I was trying to carefully explain my good news to our friends but balance that emotion. They went again to their counselor and were still told that they would not be getting visas. I got nervous again. I texted Mike that I was fearful because I thought it only fair that our friends should get their visas before we should. I went back to the embassy a day earlier than scheduled, and my counselor saw me through the glass.

"I thought I told you they won't be ready until Thursday," she said.

"Oh, okay, right. I'll come back tomorrow," I said. I nodded and politely left.

The next day, three days after Daddy arrived, he went with me to the embassy and sat outside. After twenty to thirty minutes in my counselor's office, I came out with eight sealed envelopes and my kids' visas stamped in their passports. I was speechless. Floating. There were no words.

I learned something during that final week in Sierra Leone that was so clear to me at the end of this journey. When God says it's time, then and only then is it time. And there is nothing you can do to stop it. Watching this miracle happen was almost like an out-of-body experience; it was all so unbelievable. God keeps perfect time. Until then, there is nothing you can do to make it *be* that time. And when it *is* time, it's the most exciting thing to see and watch unfold. And there's nothing you can do to stop it! For two weeks, I had heard bad news about visas and been told that I shouldn't be getting them. But I got them!

I had wasted so much energy and had so much heartache worrying. Right then, I just wanted to tell everybody to stop fretting and calm down and trust that everything was going to be fine. I wanted people to know they could stop worrying and rest. But until you get to that point yourself, that kind of quiet heart is hard to accept. This journey changed me. Very little rattles me now, which is funny because I used to get rattled so easily. I would fret about leaving the boys, fret about germs, whatever. I like me much better now.

Daddy and I rode back to the orphanage in Cherry's taxi hugging with tears running down our faces. My mind and my heart were bursting with thoughts about this miracle. *Nobody even knows how good this is! Nobody knows what just happened here! Nobody knows how good God is.* God has always got it. Just go with Him, not in front of Him, not behind Him. Just be there; be the vessel. Let Him take you and move you. Before this life journey, I thought I had to make things happen, had to plan everything, and had to stay on top of things. Like everyone else, I was always on the go, had to have the college funds, and was all about me doing, doing, doing. What can I do to change things? I was not listening, waiting.

That joy in the taxi ride back to the orphanage was mixed with such heaviness. Our friends didn't have their children's visas and had gone back to the embassy again, so we quietly told the people in the office at the center, "It really happened. I have visas." Then our friends called. Unbelievably, they got their visas, too. Their counselor said, "I'll give this to you because they gave them to your friends earlier." It was just like our oldest son's dream, the tree had fallen and the children were crossing. Then my joy was complete, and I could jump up and down, spin and yell. I called all the kids into a room and told them. It was their turn to scream and jump up and down. And, like me, they looked like deer in headlights. "Is this real? Is this really happening?" I told them, "Yes, my precious children. I'm not leaving you this time. We're *all* going home." I knew any tears shed in the airplane this time would be tears of joy.

The next day we left the orphanage before sunrise and drove about five hours to Shenge for a good-bye visit with the children's relatives and old friends. Some roads are in good condition, but most are nonexistent, with bridges made of logs lashed together. I had visited once in 2011 with a staffer from The Raining Season. And since Daddy had been on mission trips before, he pretty much knew what to expect: dirt houses with dirt floors, outside kitchens, large groups of families living together, and optional shirts for women.

The village got word we were coming and had prepared a meal. It was a celebration. The magnitude of this moment was not lost on me. Their mother never stopped smiling and came out with a huge platter of rice and goat. Daddy, the children, and I sat around the platter on cut tree stumps and wooden chairs. She poured a sauce over the food and gave Daddy and me big spoons. She never sat down. This feast was made for us and for her children. Accepting this offering and sitting there being served by her was immensely humbling. I wondered when they would eat after that. Because of that, Daddy and I didn't eat much, but enough to be polite. I'll never know the sacrifice they made for that meal. But it was apparent on her face that this meal was given joyfully. Very joyfully. That was God right there.

Though most everyone in that village speaks Sherbro, some do understand Krio or a little English. So along with a TRS staff member who spoke Krio, we walked around the village with the kids to see everybody. We stopped at every home, and all the talk was about the kids and how good and healthy they looked. All the people who spoke to me (Mommy Hayley) were very thankful, very sweet. I made sure to make eye contact with everybody and talk to everybody, touching them, smiling. That's the language I know. I had to laugh at Daddy, who brought out his Southern ways and said hello to everyone and asked, "Hey, honey, how are you?" There was a woman there who connected with Daddy and stayed with him the whole time. He thought she probably wanted to go too. As we walked, more villagers came out of their homes and followed us to the next home, and the little ones in the village liked to hold our hands. If they weren't outside already, they were coming out of their houses to see this spectacle.

Our kids stayed close. They saw some old friends but

didn't stop to play. What would they talk about? I think they were having some weird feelings of their own trying to figure out what to say. We took a lot of photos during our two hours in Shenge. I gave their birth family an album with photos of the kids and photos of me, Mike, Tyler, and Tucker. Their family. I left room for more photos, which I'd send. The Shenge visit was a celebration, a happy time. It was only when we got ready to leave that everyone's mood grew somber. The moment was here. There were quiet tears, especially from the grandparents. They might never see the children again. But we could still tell they were very pleased. The experience was just unbelievable. Amazing.

Our children weren't leaving one family and coming to another. No, our families had become one. That's my family in Shenge. We pray for them; we talk about them. We've always told the kids they have more people to love them. As hard as the three-year struggle was, it gave them time to heal and process feelings after their father's death. We've talked about going back to visit someday. Michael and I have talked a lot about all the places he wants to show me. And he wants to help. Somehow, someday, he wants to help.

A bumpy five-hour ride later, we were back at The Raining Season to spend one more night. The next day, after a lengthy good-bye ceremony there, we piled into taxis and headed for the Family Kingdom hotel, which is about ten minutes away. That was where they all received their new names and I soaked in every precious moment. Joy, Absolute joy. I counted and recounted the passports, freshly stamped with their visas. I double-checked the eight sealed envelopes from the U.S. Embassy that could only be opened by Immigration officials in the United States. I ran through all the scenarios in my head of what could go wrong the next day at the airport.

I sent short texts to Mike, telling him where we were, what we were doing, and asking him to "just pray." Back at home, my mom, Mike and the boys, our friends, Sunday school class, extended family, and numerous church families we've never met did the only thing they could do: pray. Every few hours through March 18 and 19, Mike posted a photo and name on Facebook to introduce our children, one by one. Michael, Samuel, Gabrielle, Levi, Malachi, Judah, Isaiah, and Zion. He drove Tyler to school, took Tucker to his mom's, and went to work. The house was ready; there was nothing else to do but wait. And pray.

We had breakfast at Family Kingdom, which was a big buffet-style breakfast, and the children were given coloring books. As they played on the playground, I took in every detail and was so incredibly excited watching them. I couldn't believe this was happening. In the same moment, I thought, *Okay, it's not quite over yet. I've got to get out of here.* I was excited to go to the airport and dreaded it at the same time. I talked a lot with the children that morning about what to expect. I explained that as much as they loved their new names, they would use their birth names today since those were on all the paperwork. We packed their backpacks, which included goody bags that Mike's mom, Cathy, had put together for the long airplane rides. And considering how they lost their father in a ferry accident, we also tried to prepare them for getting on the ferry that would take us to the airport.

The kids were fine on the ferry ride. Another taxi-van (a *poda*) took us to the small airport where passengers wait outside the airport to get inside after showing their passports. Daddy and I checked our two bags. That was when we started getting the looks from the employees. No one said anything to us, but they had a look of wonder about two Americans with eight kids at the airport. It was an odd sight, I'm sure. Then they checked our tickets. So far, so good.

Inside the airport, an employee looked through our passports and adoption papers. "How many kids? What are you doing?"

I explained.

"Wait, how many kids? Where's your adoption court order?"

I showed the airport employee the court orders. "This says these are my kids."

"Where do you have permission to leave with them?"

I showed the visas stamped in each of their passports.

"This is a visa. This is what tells them they can leave."

The airport employees all speak some English, but there is still a culture and language difference. How well we actually understood each other was questionable. He asked more questions, then he called another man over.

I showed them both the papers and the sealed envelopes from the U.S. Embassy. "We can't open these yet," I said.

"Why not?" they asked.

I tried to explain protocol, but actually there was no protocol because adoptions really weren't moving through Sierra Leone yet. Then our friends arrived with their kids. Other workers walked over. Here were four Americans with a total of eleven Sierra Leoneon children. About four or five workers talked, going back and forth. Daddy stayed behind me, keeping the kids together. I don't know what I would have done without him there. He watched the kids, and I focused on getting us through. I told myself to stay calm, to be nice and friendly. I had had an idea that it would probably be like this. I had my game face on: very polite but direct. I offered them more papers, even if they didn't really need them. It felt like an eternity, and my thoughts raced. *They can't really stop this because I have everything. But they could delay it and we will miss our flight.* Legally, we had everything we needed. But legally, over there, really doesn't matter. It's a totally different world.

That eternity, which in reality was about thirty minutes,

finally ended. They moved us through. I thought, *We're through! Wow!* But there would be two more hours to wait before boarding our flight to Brussels, Belgium, and my dad and I sat with the kids, keeping them quiet and busy with the goody bags. We had a meal upstairs in the airport restaurant that, oddly enough, served mac and cheese and burgers. I texted Mike to let him know we were through and to keep praying. Daddy held and played with the kids and prayed quietly, "God, You've got this." Finally we got outside to board the plane where they do a final security screening.

> I had my game face on: very polite but direct. I offered them more papers, even if they didn't really need them. It felt like an eternity, and my thoughts raced.

As the lady screened Gabrielle and me, and the men screened the boys, we could tell they were talking about us in Krio. Walking out to the plane, my excitement bubbled up. Climbing the stairs to that jumbo jet was like climbing the stairs to heaven. "Look at the engine," I showed them. "Look at the airplane wings." Once inside the plane, we got the kids buckled in, and I started to relax just a bit. The children, especially the little ones, were amazed, looking at everything. Little fingers couldn't help but push the buttons again and again on the TVs in the seat backs. They probably had to buy a new airplane seat where Zion sat.

As we waited for everyone else to board (another eternity), I kept worrying and waiting for someone to get on the plane and try to delay us. I think I've seen too many movies. Then we talked to the kids about how takeoff would make them feel. At last we were up! Above the clouds, some of them didn't like looking out the window and instead fidgeted with buttons.

After all these years, this was the first time I'd left Sierra Leone happy.

Even then, up in the air, I couldn't relax until I was fairly sure we were out of Sierra Leone airspace. I looked back at our friends. "We're out of the country!" I could breathe. I could have sung. Yes, it happened. My children and I were going home! After a six and a half hour flight to Brussels, we settled down in the airport during the layover before our next flight to Washington, DC. Of course, no one could sleep. We boarded a jet, and in another eight hours and forty-five minutes, we landed in DC the next day. The flight attendants took a group photo with us, and the pilot made an announcement as we were landing welcoming the Jones family home to America. It was a thrilling moment! And thanks to a member of Congress, the flag that flew over the United States Capitol on the day we landed, March 19, 2013, was flown in honor of Michael, Samuel, Gabrielle, Levi, Malachi, Judah, Isaiah, and Zion. We have the flag and the certificate welcoming them home to the USA. We felt extremely honored and so blessed by God to orchestrate such events.

As we stood in the line labeled "not U.S. citizens," my mind started working again. What if someone at the embassy had missed a piece of paperwork in those sealed envelopes? What then? But we were in our own country, so it had to be okay. We went into a room off to the side where Immigration officials opened the envelopes, and I tried to keep the kids calm as Daddy had to go through the other line labeled "U.S. citizens." They called Michael up, then Samuel, to ask a few questions. They asked me a few questions. It took longer than I thought it would, but all was well. Daddy, the kids, and I had to hustle to make our connection to Nashville.

That final hour-long flight was nothing but excitement, joy, and giddiness. I texted Erica:

> I can't wait to talk to you. Oh, how I love you so. I just had my release in the last seat of the tiny airplane going to Nashville. Feels like I'm born again . . . feels like I'm living for the very first time. I know that I know this is exactly where I'm supposed to be, how it was supposed to happen. I know God really does love me. Good things are for me too. I wasn't just called to suffer. I have crossed the desert. Glory

to God in the Highest. Holy, Holy is His name above every other name.

I couldn't believe He had done this. I was so happy I honestly didn't know what to say to God during that flight. I just praised Him. We were spread all over the plane, so Daddy and I sat separately to keep an eye on the kids. Nashville International Airport allowed Mike, Tucker, and Tyler to get boarding passes to meet us at the gate along with two local media outlets. Getting off the plane, the first thing I saw were cameras. Tucker held his poster board sign that my mom had helped him make, which said, "I'm the little brother." Our group descended on Mike, who had a bouquet of flowers for me. All I could say was, "We're home!" Once the other passengers waiting for connections realized what was going on, they all burst into applause as we hugged, kissed, and hugged some more.

> I'm sure we did just the opposite of good advice for new adoptees: don't overwhelm them. The kids would have been highly disappointed if people weren't there to welcome them.

For a few seconds, Tucker, four at the time, shyly hid from his brothers and sister even though they had seen each other numerous times on Skype. But this was real. He said, "Hi." And they said, "Hi." Language was still an issue. Then that timidity ended. They grabbed hands and started walking. Gabrielle held Tucker's hand, and Tyler held Zion's hand. I'd forgotten my purse on the plane, so Daddy ran back to get it. I kept looking back as we made our way down the terminal to make sure I still had everybody. Momma Hayley and her ducks.

I had no idea how many people would be there cheering, waving balloons and signs. I was floored. I'm sure we did just the opposite of good advice for new adoptees: don't overwhelm them, don't make a huge fuss. But people were finally able to see these kids they had heard about and prayed for over the past three years. And, yes, I wanted them to be seen. They were here! Honestly, I think the kids would have been highly disappointed if people weren't there to welcome them. So much of that night is a blur, but I remember talking to my teacher friends who were holding a sign that read, "We're lovin' the Jones Dozen." We hugged Mike's parents, my mom and dad, my Sunday school class, and gave interviews to local media. Running on adrenalin and airplane catnaps, I have no idea what I said.

My mom says she will never forget seeing my kids' faces. Someone took the sweetest photo of Mom with her hands on Gabrielle's shoulders as they looked into each other's eyes for the first time.

"I thought I was going to burst," she told me. It was an immediate love and connection. "Where have they been all of our lives?"

Conclusion

The Jones Dozen

(Hayley)

God humbles us every day. Every single day. I have done absolutely nothing in my life that makes me worthy to see God move every day. Yet I do. This journey gave me a totally different view of God. I thought I was called to suffer and be strong in the suffering. I accepted that. But God really does give good gifts. Our ten children are the cherry on top that never ends.

Whether it is in finances and provision, or in the redemption and healing of a young, once-shattered heart, I see God move constantly. Though the children have been home two years now, I still think about the miracle of them getting here and my mind is blown. The joy is still unspeakable. God brought order to our lives when the Great Eight came home. You'd think having ten kids is chaos, well, the real chaos were those three years of waiting, working, praying, and crying. He calmed the storm when He brought them home.

Life here at the Jones house is not always easy. We have had our growing pains. Bringing in eight children to join a family of four and incorporating two very different cultures has many challenges. But they are just that, challenges to overcome. The children came home, and we hunkered down for the first few months establishing our family, building relationships, learning expectations, and letting each find their role.

Michael and Gabrielle have Skyped with their birth mother when she was able to make the long ride to Freetown. I was so worried about how it would go the first time. Would she be sad? No, she was beaming. She got to meet Tucker, and the children showed her our house by walking around with the laptop. She saw their bedrooms, their favorite toys, and where I cook each day. She laughed and smiled and just seemed so proud of them. Like they'd been chosen. Yes, they have. God chooses each of us. I prayed every night during the three years of waiting that God would make this transition smooth. God has gone above and beyond my prayer. I continuously ask God to put His hedge of protection around our family, to not allow Satan to sift us like wheat, for I know he wanders the earth like a roaring lion looking to steal, kill, and destroy (Luke 22:31; 1 Peter 5:8; John 10:10).

Mike's parents and brother, Brian, and his family are just two and three doors down, and my parents live a few miles away. Love was immediate, and their relationships have grown quickly. My dad, whom the kids call Poppy, hugs, wrestles, and kicks the soccer ball with them when he can on weekends. My mom, whom the kids call Mimi, remembers the first time she took Gabrielle to the mall and how she stared at everything. Mom loved that day and laughs now about how Gabby knew exactly what kind of clothes she likes. Mike's parents, Cathy (Yay Yay) and Grandpa Ken, see the kids almost daily, and Tyler spends time with Yay Yay everyday after school. Brian's wife, Krista, a cosmetologist, has helped with Gabrielle's hair. Our oldest boys, Michael and Samuel, go to the Joneses so they can watch soccer on DirecTV since we don't have that or cable. When the kids first came home, my parents' neighborhood collected bicycles for all of them. Again, we are completely humbled by the giving of others.

Michael and Gabrielle have Skyped with their birth mother when she was able to make the long ride to Freetown. I was so worried about how it would go the first time. Would she be sad? No, she was beaming.

Our Thanksgivings and Christmases are thirty-plus people and full of food, football, and crafts. During Thanksgiving 2014, Mike's grandpa, Paw Paw Cox, had just gotten out of the hospital, was weak, and didn't quite have his voice back. Samuel, who's so quiet and loving, went over to Paw Paw's chair four or five times to pat him, give him a hug, and check on him.

Both of Mike's grandmothers lived another year after the children came home. In March 2014, when Granny Cox was about to go to heaven, all the children were there in the waiting area with Paw Paw. Michael asked if he could pray. We gathered around holding hands, and Michael prayed the sweetest, most wonderful prayer in his thick accent. Months later at Thanksgiving, Paw Paw whispered, "I want Michael to do the prayer." On the way home, Paw Paw, who is a minister, told Yay Yay, "I wouldn't be surprised if Michael is called to ministry."

Throughout our three-year journey, we had umpteen Sunday school classes from at least three churches praying for us. Today, Mike's late-Granny Cox's ladies group at their small church collects fifty dollars just about every month, a sweet gift, which Paw Paw brings to me. It's obedience blessed, and that is pure joy.

God told Mike he would provide for us. He has. He will. We trust. To this day, our budget never works on paper. Mike pays the bills every Sunday night, and then he puts it away.

God told Mike he would provide for us. He *has*. He *will*. We trust. To this day, our budget never works on paper. Mike pays the bills every Sunday night, and then he puts it away. If we examined and thought and worried about money, we would go insane. If something breaks, Mike fixes it. He will tackle anything, including installing new windows on the house or changing a transmission in the car. We have enough. It's just like manna from heaven. In Exodus 16, God sends down bread from heaven to feed His people. It is just enough for the day. Nothing extra can be kept because He wants His people to rely solely on Him. That's what we have to do. When we rely on Him, that's when we can really experience God's blessings.

Sometimes people will tell me their two or three kids wear them out, so how in the world do I handle ten? My true answer to them: God's been good. He's gives enough strength for each day. Enough. Always enough.

In 2014, we spent an average of $575 per week on groceries and toiletries. Add that up, and that's about $30,000 annually. We shop at Aldi, Walmart, and Sam's Club to buy in bulk. We buy fifty-pound bags of rice and several ten-pound sacks of potatoes. Planning meals for a dozen every day sounds overwhelming. But I just put my big girl pants on and do it. A typical dinner might be two crockpots of lasagna or my version of a Sierra Leoneon dish, groundnut soup and rice. Dinner almost always includes rice or noodles, and there are never leftovers. And now Gabrielle, through her homeschool tutorial, is learning to cook—and she's really good at it.

When it comes to educating our oldest three children,

we felt that placing them in public school without filling the educational gaps would be detrimental to them. You wouldn't build your house if chunks of the foundation were missing. Homeschooling them has been the best way for them to focus and get caught up, and we have really enjoyed it. The other seven children are doing well in our local elementary school, and we have been blessed by all of their teachers. We will continue to let God lead us when it comes to decisions about their education.

Homework is done at our huge, picnic-style table, and the kids head off to play after. If it's nice outside, you know they're out looking for critters or playing soccer. Days are busy, but I wouldn't have it any other way. When Mike gets home, homework is finished and an everyday dinner sees all twelve of us around that table. Afterward, two children take care of the dishes, others wipe the table, and some vacuum before showers and a family devotional, which has become our favorite time of the day. Once the older boys are in bed by ten thirty or so, it takes me a little while to wind down, so sleep might come around midnight. Mike jokes that he gets to go to work and rest while my day never stops.

Each child gets to choose one after-school activity. This doesn't seem like much . . . until you have ten kids. During the 2014–15 school year, nine played soccer and Tyler started taking piano lessons, which he really enjoys. In the spring and fall we spend every week night chauffeuring children around to practices and games. It takes a village. Grandparents help with chauffeuring and fast-food runs ordered off of the dollar menu, which we know by heart. At McDonald's, all of us eat for $27.98 and drink water. During soccer seasons, Saturdays are spent at the soccer field going from one field to another watching the children play. There are days we just have to hug and hold each other a minute, then let go and start running again! We get to sleep thirty to forty-five minutes extra on Saturday and Sundays, and that definitely is our recharge time. We both are drained more than we thought we could ever endure, but one look in a child's face and we're good. We don't have time to think about much else but what's next, let's go, got to get this done, and next!

Never at a loss for words, Mike calls me "the tortilla wrap to our Jones family burrito." He says, "If it wasn't for her we would be spilled all over the plate!" Sure, there are days when I am tired. Tired from cooking for twelve people every day, tired from several loads of laundry every day, from the busyness. But I'm not tired *of* it. This is what I waited for; this is what I prayed for. Yes, I am tired of repeating myself a thousand times and can't even count how many times a day I hear, "Mom! Mom!" An uninterrupted shower or going to the bathroom without a knock on the door would be lovely. But if I never heard a voice say, "Mom" again or heard the sound of feet running down the hall, I would be devastated beyond words. Perspective. Perspective changes everything.

When we were looking for a house in 2004, we had looked in neighborhoods, but eventually found the house we're in now, on a country road. We know a neighborhood wouldn't have worked. Tyler and Isaiah love to look for critters in the creek. We need our 10.4 acres for riding bikes or playing soccer. The kids came home in spring 2013, and by that fall, we had all ten playing soccer on a rec league with shoes we found at Goodwill. Growing up in Sierra Leone, they played barefoot street soccer, so they all had to get used to wearing soccer cleats. Michael has really taken to the game and was given a scholarship to play on a travel soccer team.

We stand amazed at miracles every day. People we have never met before have blessed our family. I can't tell you how many times a stranger has come up to us in the parking lot of a grocery store and handed us a gift card or cash. They'll say they don't know why, but felt led. Two acquaintances said they wanted to give us beef to fill our freezer. We were thrilled; meat is expensive. We plugged in an old freezer we had and, of course, it didn't work. We worried what we would do with all that meat we would receive because we couldn't afford to buy a new freezer. We didn't say a word about it to anyone. A few days later, a lady from an appliance store called and said, "Someone has just paid for you a freezer of your choice. We just need to know which one you want." Mike almost dropped the phone. God did it again. Only He knew what we needed. We have learned to live by what we need, not what we want.

Another person from church heard we needed computers for homeschooling Michael, Samuel, and Gabrielle. I had never even seen this man before, and he gave us five hundred dollars toward a computer. I searched Craigslist for a used laptop and bought one for that price. The seller asked what it would be used for, so I told her about our family. I met her at the Apple store, and she had the entire Microsoft suite installed. To top it off, two weeks later she called and said she forgot to give me something for the computer and could we meet again. When I met her, she handed me another used Mac and said, "My husband needed another computer anyway and I know you really needed another one so here's his old computer." God doubled the offering.

A dentist covered what insurance doesn't pay for the kids' first dental visits. We still have a lot of dental needs from years of neglect, and they all need orthodontic corrections. God knows our needs and what we can and can't live without. I don't want to do anything unless God tells me to do it. And I know He'll lead us in the right direction because He's proven it so many times. When I pray it's not just a casual, "I'll pray about it." I pray now with thanksgiving. I *know* He will answer.

We were blessed with our first family vacation, which

we thought would never be possible! My mother's middle school art teacher heard about our family and planned and organized an entire weeklong trip to Amelia Island in Florida. We had a beach house, beach toys, fireworks, fishing poles, disposable cameras for each child, hats and shirts with our names on them, lunches and dinners in restaurants—real restaurants where you sit down at a table and order food not on a dollar menu. It was the Great Eight's first time in a real restaurant in the United States. They loved it! She had fun activities planned like bike riding through the park, a horse and carriage ride, toys from a local toy store, a boat ride around the island, and even a date night for Mike and me. On the last night, people gathered in the park for a shrimp boil to bid us farewell. Thinking back on that trip, I am still speechless about the love and sacrifice from that community for our family. This was a lesson for the children and us.

Not only do we get to witness the miracles of provision, we also get a first-row seat in the miracles of redemption. God's will was not for our children to have ever been orphans . . . but they were. So God took that pain and those lost and broken years and suffering and He made something beautiful out of it. That's what redemption is. Turning something broken into something beautiful. We have spent many late nights listening to hours of past hurts and traumas. We have had some of the deepest conversations at some of the most random times. There are many stories and memories our children have that their American-born friends and families will never have to deal with or even think about. We walk this road by the grace of God. I know many people want to know what the children think and how they are doing. I will not speak for them, but I can give you their words that were written in a letter to us.

> Thank you for all that you have done for our family. I know it is really hard to take care of ten kids. We are really grateful to be a part of this family. I pray the Lord will continue to provide. I am grateful to be here because I know what my life should have been in Sierra Leone. Thank you for teaching me how to live Christ like and not to follow the way of other people. We cannot repay you for all that you are doing for us. There is not even a word to repay you. You are the best parents I have seen in my life. I will never forget the first time we spoke to you. That was the best moment in my life. May God bless you, Mom and Dad. I love you so much.

That is redemption. That is the love of God. They have dreams to help others and make a difference in this world. I know they will. God has big plans for them. They pray for far-away friends and family. They pray for Salone. We all pray for God's protection on the center and their village, both of which were on lockdown for months during the Ebola epidemic.

All of these blessings are God's reminders to us not to worry. He's got this! That's the biggest confirmation we receive when walking in obedience to what He has asked us to do. Through this long journey, we have learned many things, but they all come down to this: When God calls you to do something, go for it, all the way. Have faith. He will see you through, and His timing is absolutely perfect.

So no matter why you despair, know this: God will prevail. Tie a knot at the end of your rope and hang tight. You don't need a savior unless you need to be saved from something. You don't need a redeemer unless you need to be redeemed from something. You can't fully experience God without getting refined in the fire by Him, and you will never, ever be the same. The deeper the valley and darker the night, the more joy you will feel when the light comes and you reach the mountaintop. Oh, His amazing grace, how sweet the sound that saved a wretch like me. I once was lost, but now I'm found. I was blind before, but now I see.

Children's Profiles

Including text from Hayley's papers that she read to the children the day they left the orphanage.

Michael Thomas

Michael means "Who is like the Lord?" The archangel who is a warrior and leader of the angel armies (Jude 1:9; Revelation 12:7–9). As the oldest you have been a leader to your family. Your devotion to God makes you a warrior. As our oldest son, you have been given the name of your father, a special rite for the eldest son. Thomas is a family name. The name of Hayley's mom's great uncle and the name of her dad's great uncle.

Michael is the eldest of the ten, whom all of the children follow. He is admired by his siblings for being strong and confident, but he is also caring and patient. He is a leader and stays true to what he believes in. He makes us proud by the wise decisions he makes. He has a heart to help the poor and the lost. Soccer is his love and his gift. He is loud and joyous most all the time. He is rarely seen not smiling or laughing. He does his best no matter what his task. Though his life has been full of tragedies, by the grace of God he has come through it all with a happy countenance.

Samuel Titus

Samuel means "God heard." He was the son who was prayed for and God answered. The story of Samuel can be found in 1 and 2 Samuel. We have prayed for you and God has answered. Titus means "pleasing." Your kind heart and gentle, loving nature led us to this name for you.

Samuel is quiet and observant. He is soft-spoken around others but makes his family laugh with his funny jokes and humorous personality. He is always willing to help and is aware of how others are feeling. He has suffered much and overcome.

Gabrielle Grace

Gabrielle means "Woman of God." The feminine form of Gabriel, one of the seven archangels. He was the angel who announced the birth of Jesus to Mary. Your faith and prayers during this time demonstrate you are a woman of God. Grace means "Favor." Though only 5 letters long, this word has so much meaning. As a child of God you have received His favor, His amazing grace. You once were lost, but now you are found. Grace is also a family name. It is the name of your great-grandmother.

Gabrielle is the sister to nine brothers. She is sensitive to the feelings of others and is loving and nurturing and eager to learn new things. She loves crafts, sewing, shopping, and cooking, yet she can hang with boys playing soccer, four-wheeling, and tromping through the woods. She is a gift giver and wants to make her family feel special.

Levi Peter

Levi means "pledged or joined." Levi was one of Jacob's 12 sons and was the father of the tribe assigned to priestly duties. Now you have "joined" our family forever. They say people with this name tend to be creative and are drawn to the arts. This could not be truer of you. You are an artist yourself! Peter means "Rock." Jesus gave this name to Simon because he saw not only who he was but also who he would become. Peter became a solid rock in the days of the early church.

Levi is usually quiet and is more reserved than some of his other brothers. He is quite the talented artist and often draws and paints pictures for his family. He will also lay on the couch and read books if he gets the chance. Levi enjoys playing soccer and works hard at getting better.

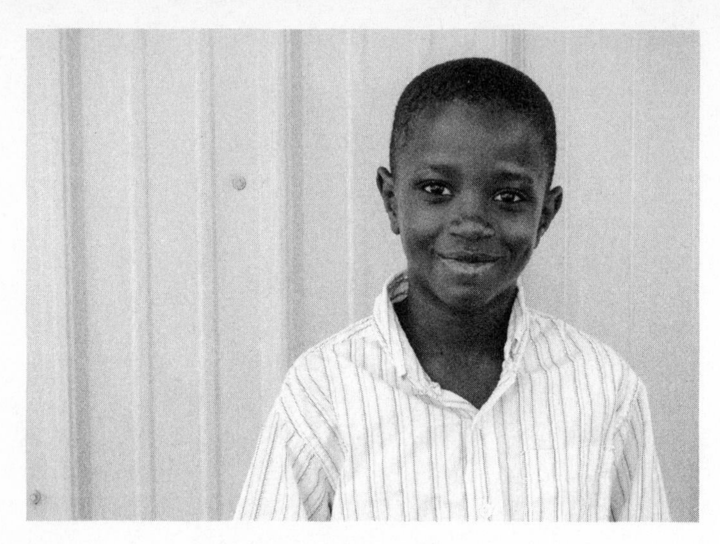

Malachi Drake

Malachi means "messenger of God." This is you! You can quote more Scripture than anyone I know! You say Scripture while you play. You ride your bike calling out Scripture. You are a messenger of God! Malachi was the name of a prophet in Jerusalem. You can read about him in the book of Malachi. Drake is a family name. This is Mom's maiden name, the surname of her family. It is very special for you to carry this name.

Malachi is smart and intense. The only time he stops is in his sleep, but even then he talks. He memorizes almost everything he reads and can quote many Bible verses. He is loud and expresses all his emotions. He likes to please his family and is always willing to help out when needed.

Tyler Deacon

He is his own little person. He loves to be outdoors finding critters, tromping through the woods, and riding his bicycle or four-wheeler. He went from being the oldest of two children to being right in the middle of ten. He has had his struggles but has found his place and enjoys all the company. Tyler has a love for music, especially the piano, and enjoys his lessons. He has quite an imagination and writes his own books for his family to read. He has his mother's sensitivity to others but also her sense of humor. He is his mother's child.

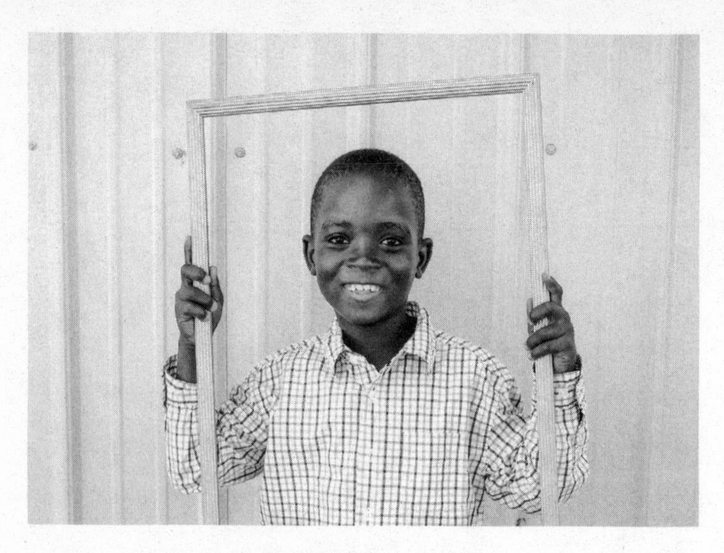

Judah Currell

Judah means "I will praise the Lord." Judah was one of the 12 tribes of Israel. David and Jesus were born of this tribe. We "praise the Lord" for you. Your strength is one of the reasons we gave you this name. Currell is a family name. This was your great-grandfather's name. He was very special to us and loved by many.

Judah seems to make those who know him smile. Maybe it's his deep voice, his bright smile, or his loud laugh, but he has a great personality, and his classmates love him. He gets his name chanted in class and around home almost daily. "Ju-dah, Ju-dah!" It never seems to get old. He is fun to joke with and very loving to his family. Judah is a happy-go-lucky kind of boy.

Isaiah William

Isaiah means "salvation of God; the Lord helps me." The Lord has helped you; watched over you and us. Isaiah was also one of the Major Prophets in the Old Testament. You can read about him in the book of Isaiah. William is a family name. Many men in our family bear this name—your grandfather and two of your great-grandfathers. They are honored to share this name with you!

Isaiah is a ball of energy and full of questions. He has a sweet disposition and has many friends. He will dress up as superheroes with Tucker, find critters in the yard with Tyler, play soccer with his big brothers, and eat more than anyone I know. He keeps his family laughing with his quirky ways.

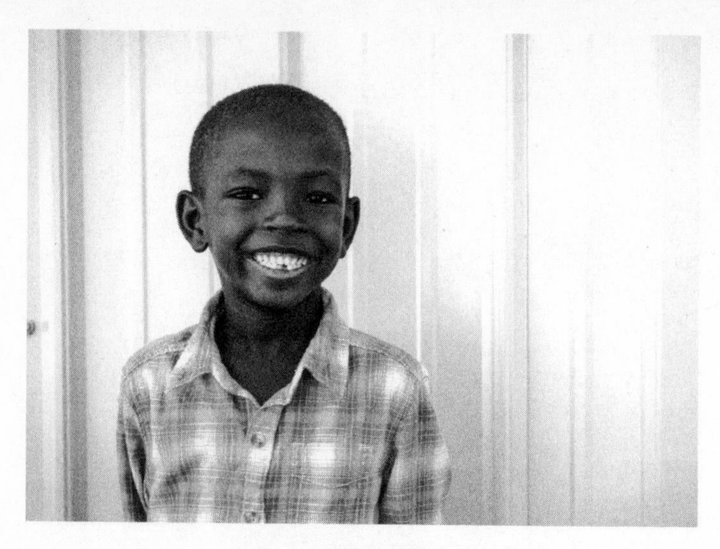

Zion Davidson

Zion is used in the Bible to represent Jerusalem and heaven. It says Jesus will return for His people in the end on Mt. Zion. You are the youngest, the end of our Great 8. You are strong and beautiful. For these reasons, we chose this name for you. Davidson is a family name. This is the surname of your great grandparents. It is very special for you to carry this name.

Zion wakes up with full steam every morning and never slows down. He is bouncy and energetic, just like Tigger. He is loving and sweet natured. Zion plays soccer with the boys and tries to keep up with them, and he likes to snuggle with mom at the end of each day.

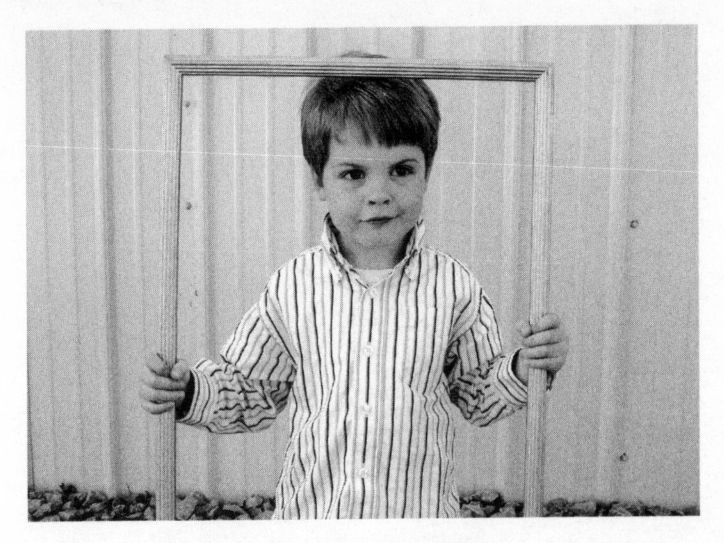

Tucker Derby

He is his father's child. He looks like Mike and acts like Mike. He is a boy who knows just what he wants. He is shy with those he doesn't know but never stops talking at home. His age doesn't matter to him; he thinks he can do what the big boys do. Tucker likes to be right in the middle of the action. You never know what superhero or character he may dress as each day. He has a great imagination and is fun to be around. He adores Michael and has a special bond with him; they are two peas in a pod.

Acknowledgments

There are so many people who have impacted our lives: our family, Ken and Cathy Jones, Bill and Susan Drake, Rev. William A. Cox, Joey and Courtney Lankford, Brian and Krista Jones, and all our friends. We thank you and we love you. Thank you for continuing to journey with us making the sweetest of memories.

Those families who walked this adoption journey with us, who went to the hard places right beside us, you know who you are. Our hearts are forever grateful for your love, your understanding, and your friendship.

To the Greene's, who were a pillar when the ground seemed so shaky, thank you for being examples of faith.

Thanks to all people who have blessed and continue to bless our family. It truly takes a village to raise a child. We have many people to thank for the selfless acts they have shown our family. God knows who you all are, and we thank Him for you. Thank you to the teachers who pour out their love on our children and care for them as their own.

To the Sunday school classes who prayed us through good and bad days, thank you for your kindness and support.

To our church, Grace Chapel in Leiper's Fork, thank you for being the body of Christ, for standing firmly on God's Word and pouring out love on our family.

Thank you, God, for giving us a story to share. May it bring You honor.

If you enjoyed this book, will you consider sharing the message with others?

- Mention the book in a Facebook post, Twitter update, Pinterest pin, blog post, or upload a picture through Instagram.
- Recommend this book to those in your small group, book club, workplace, and classes.
- Head over to facebook.com/worthypublishing, "LIKE" the page, and post a comment as to what you enjoyed the most.
- Tweet "I recommend reading #AtAnyCost by @JonesDozen // @worthypub"
- Pick up a copy for someone you know who would be challenged and encouraged by this message.
- Write a book review online.

You can subscribe to Worthy Publishing's newsletter at worthypublishing.com.

WORTHY PUBLISHING FACEBOOK PAGE

WORTHY PUBLISHING WEBSITE